WRITERS AND THEIR WORK

ISOBEL ARMSTRONG
*General Editor*

# MIDDLETON
AND HIS COLLABORATORS

© *Copyright RSC. Photograph by Stephen Vaughan*

RSC, 2005. *A New Way to Please You* (or *The Old Law*) by Thomas Middleton and William Rowley (c.1618). Directed by Sean Holmes, designed by Kandis Cook.

Seated in background: Geoffrey Freshwater as Creon; standing: Julian Stolzenberg as Courtier; seated in foreground: John Foster as Courtier, Jonjo O'Neill as Simonedes.

WW

# MIDDLETON AND HIS COLLABORATORS

Mark Hutchings
and
A. A. Bromham

© Copyright 2008 by Mark Hutchings and A. A. Bromham
First published in 2008 by Northcote House Publishers Ltd,
Horndon, Tavistock, Devon, PL19 9NQ, United Kingdom.
Tel: +44 (0) 1822 810066  Fax: +44 (0) 1822 810034.

All rights reserved. No part of this work may be reproduced or stored in an information retrieval system (other than short extracts for the purposes of review) without the express permission of the Publishers given in writing.

**British Library Cataloguing-in-Publication Data**
A catalogue record for this book is available from the British Library

ISBN 978-0-7463-1075-5 hardcover
iSBN 978-0-7463-1080-9 paperback
Typeset by PDQ Typesetting, Newcastle-under-Lyme
Printed and bound in the United Kingdom

In Memory of Zara Bruzzi

# Contents

| | |
|---|---|
| *Chronology* | viii |
| *Preface and Acknowledgements* | xi |
| *A Question of Attribution* | xiii |
| *Abbreviations and References* | xiv |
| Introduction | 1 |
| 1. Middleton | 5 |
| 2. Collaboration | 25 |
| 3. Middleton and Dekker | 39 |
| 4. Middleton and Shakespeare | 54 |
| 5. Middleton and Rowley | 73 |
| 6. Intertextual Middleton | 88 |
| Afterword | 98 |
| *Notes* | 100 |
| *Select Bibliography* | 110 |
| *Index* | 119 |

# Chronology

| | |
|---|---|
| 1580 | Thomas Middleton born. First son of William and Anne Middleton. Baptized 18 April in St Lawrence Jewry. |
| 1586 | Father dies (January). Mother marries Thomas Harvey (November). |
| 1597 | *The Wisdom of Solomon Paraphrased* (poem; published in spring). |
| 1598 | Matriculates at Queen's College, Oxford (April). |
| 1599 | *Microcynicon: Six Snarling Satires* (poem; publicly burned in June). |
| 1600 | *The Ghost of Lucrece* (poem). |
| 1601 | Leaves Oxford without a degree and is reported to be 'daylie accompanynge the players' in London. |
| 1602 | **Collaboration with Dekker, Drayton, Munday and Webster**: *Caesar's Fall; or Two Shapes* (play; Admiral's Men; lost). |
| | *The Chester Tragedy* (first play Middleton writes independently; Admiral's Men; lost). |
| c.1603 | Marries Magdalen (Mary) Marbecke. |
| c.1604 | Son, Edward, born. |
| 1604 | **Collaboration with Dekker and Jonson**: *The Magnificent Entertainment* (pageant; contributes the speech of Zeal). |
| | *The Phoenix* (play; Children of Paul's). |
| | **Collaboration with Dekker**: *1 Honest Whore* (play; Prince Henry's Men). |
| | *The Ant and the Nightingale, or Father Hubbard's Tales* (pamphlet). |
| | *The Black Book* (pamphlet). |

|  |  |
|---|---|
|  | **Collaboration with Dekker**. *News from Gravesend* (pamphlet). |
|  | **Collaboration with Dekker**. *The Meeting of Gallants at an Ordinary* (pamphlet). |
|  | *Michaelmas Term* (play; Children of Paul's). |
| 1605 | *A Trick to Catch the Old One* (play; Children of Paul's). |
|  | *A Mad World, My Masters* (play; Children of Paul's). |
|  | *A Yorkshire Tragedy* (play; King's Men). Possible collaboration with Shakespeare. |
| 1605–6 | **Collaboration with Shakespeare**: *Timon of Athens* (play; King's Men). |
| 1606 | *The Viper and Her Brood* (lost). |
|  | *The Puritan, or the Widow of Watling Street* (play; Children of Paul's). |
|  | *The Revenger's Tragedy* (play; King's Men). |
| 1607 | *Your Five Gallants* (play; Children of the Chapel). |
| 1608–9 | **Collaboration with Dekker**: *The Bloody Banquet* (play; Beeston's Boys). |
| 1608 | Moves with his family to Newington Butts, Southwark. |
| 1609 | *Sir Robert Sherley's Entertainment in Cracovia* (pamphlet). |
|  | *The Two Gates of Salvation* (pamphlet; reprinted in 1620 as *The Marriage of the Old and the New Testament*, and in 1627 as *God's Parliament House*). |
| 1611 | **Collaboration with Dekker**: *The Roaring Girl* (play; Prince Henry's Men). |
|  | *No Wit, No Help Like a Woman's* (play; Prince Henry's Men). |
|  | *The Lady's Tragedy* (*Second Maiden's Tragedy*) (play; King's Men). Possibly revised by Shakespeare. |
| 1613 | *A Chaste Maid in Cheapside* (play; Lady Elizabeth's Men with the Children of the Queen's Revels). |
|  | *The New River Entertainment* (pageant). |
|  | *The Triumphs of Truth* (pageant; Grocers' Company). |
|  | **Collaboration with Rowley**: *Wit at Several Weapons* (play; Prince Charles's Men). |
| 1614 | *The Masque of Cupid* (masque; lost). |
|  | *More Dissemblers Besides Women* (play; King's Men). |
| c.1615–16 | **Adaptation of Shakespeare**: *Macbeth* (play; King's Men). |
| c.1616 | *The Widow* (play; King's Men). |
|  | *The Witch* (play; King's Men). |

| | |
|---|---|
| 1616 | *Civitatis Amor* (pageant).<br>**Collaboration with Rowley**: *A Fair Quarrel* (play; Prince Charles's Men). |
| 1617 | *The Triumphs of Honour and Industry* (pageant; Grocers' Company). |
| 1618 | *The Peacemaker* (pamphlet).<br>**Collaboration with Rowley (and Massinger?/Heywood?)**: *The Old Law* (play; Prince Charles's Men). |
| 1619 | *The Inner Temple Masque*, or *The Masque of Heroes* (masque; Inner Temple).<br>*The Triumphs of Love and Antiquity* (pageant; Skinners' Company). |
| 1620 | **Collaboration with Rowley**: *The World Tossed at Tennis* (masque; Prince Charles's Men).<br>*Hengist, King of Kent* (play; King's Men).<br>*Honourable Entertainments* (pageants; April 1620–April 1621).<br>Middleton appointed City Chronologer. |
| c.1621 | *Women Beware Women* (play; King's Men). |
| 1621 | **Adaptation of Shakespeare**: *Measure for Measure* (play; King's Men).<br>*The Sun in Aries* (pageant; Drapers' Company).<br>**Collaboration with Webster**: *Anything for a Quiet Life* (play; King's Men). |
| 1622 | **Collaboration with Rowley**: *The Changeling* (play; Lady Elizabeth's Men).<br>**Collaboration with Fletcher?**: *The Nice Valour* (play; King's Men?).<br>*The Triumphs of Honour and Virtue* (pageant; Grocers' Company). |
| 1623 | **Collaboration with Rowley, Dekker and Ford**: *The Spanish Gypsy* (play; Lady Elizabeth's Men).<br>*The Triumphs of Integrity* (pageant; Drapers' Company). |
| 1624 | *A Game at Chess* (play; King's Men).<br>*The Triumphs of Health and Prosperity* (pageant; Drapers' Company). |
| 1626 | Pageant for the entry of the king and queen (unperformed). |
| 1627 | Middleton dies. Buried 4 July, Newington Butts, Southwark. |

# Preface and Acknowledgements

> While the word is in your mouth it is your own,
> when it is once spoken it is another's.
>
> (Tilley, *Dictionary of Proverbs*, 1950)

It is axiomatic that all writing – and reading – is intertextual: 'etymologically, the text is a tissue, a woven fabric',[1] formed out of materials used elsewhere and reworked. The composition of a text, and its interpretations, calls up numerous other texts in a potentially endless chain of association. This is perhaps nowhere more evident than in the early modern theatre, whose owners, censors, writers, actors, playgoers, printers, patrons, readers, attackers, defenders, all contributed to a rich palimpsest of signification that continues to excite their modern counterparts. To take the three most obvious players in this list: writer, actor and playgoer all collaborate in bringing plays to life. All three, that is, call up myriad texts in the writing, performing and witnessing of a play. This study examines the career of a playwright whose name is almost synonymous with 'collaboration', and explores how the term might be usefully applied, locally and more generally, to early modern playmaking.

A book about collaboration is also, most obviously in this case, a collaborative enterprise. It would be inappropriate, but also inaccurate, to assign portions or shares of this book to either contributor. At numerous points in its making we collaboratively reworked and refashioned our material, to produce a text that, not unlike many early modern texts, associates two or more names. During the course of the project we have benefited from the knowledge and advice of a number of scholars. We would like to thank Gary Taylor (University of Alabama) and John Jowett

(Shakespeare Institute, University of Birmingham), editors of the Oxford Middleton project, Richard Dutton (University of Ohio), Andrew Gurr (University of Reading), Michela Calore, Sue Wiseman (Birkbeck College, London) and Edel Lamb (Queen's University, Belfast). We are grateful to Sam Walters, Artistic Director of The Orange Tree Theatre, Richmond-upon-Thames, for information about his 1992 production of John Marston's *The Dutch Courtesan*.

In writing about collaboration we have become acutely aware of the difficulty of laying sole claim to the authorship of anything one writes, and of the extent to which it has been influenced and shaped by so many people. Among them it is appropriate here to acknowledge especially the late Margot Heinemann, and, above all, the late Zara Bruzzi: years of teaching Renaissance literature with her, of collaborative research and shared interests, mean that she is a presence throughout the book. In particular, the section from Chapter 6 on Daniel, Shakespeare, Middleton and Rowley derives in part from unpublished work carried out with her. Despite the ways in which 'collaboration', interpreted broadly, may conceal the traces of influences, the faults that remain are our own.

# A Question of Attribution

The convenient shorthand of identifying a play with its author(s) is misleading because collaboration complicates the entire concept of 'intellectual ownership'. Early modern writers in general, and dramatists in particular, did not enjoy the kind of authority 'authorship' confers. Yet scholarship is understandably concerned with establishing an authorial canon from the surviving evidence; only comparatively recently has one of the greatest plays of the age, *The Revenger's Tragedy*, been assigned to Thomas Middleton, while his close relationship with Thomas Dekker has led to intermittent claims for one or both writing *Blurt, Master Constable* and *The Family of Love*. This study follows the latest scholarship in its attributions, but, as will become clear, its interest in attribution studies is incidental: we propose that the processes of collaboration that brought plays to fruition are a more accurate measure of early modern playmaking.

# Abbreviations and References

C.  Thomas Middleton, *The Changeling*, in Middleton, *Five Plays*, ed. Brian Loughrey and Neil Taylor (London: Penguin, 1988)
CMC  Thomas Middleton, *A Chaste Maid in Cheapside*, in Middleton, *Five Plays*, ed. Brian Loughrey and Neil Taylor (London: Penguin, 1988)
CR  Samuel Daniel, *The Complaint of Rosamond*, in *Elizabethan Verse Romances*, ed. M. M. Reese (London: Routledge, 1968)
DC  John Marston, *The Dutch Courtesan*, ed. Gamini Salgado (Harmondsworth: Penguin, 1975)
FQ  Thomas Middleton, *A Fair Quarrel*, ed. R. V. Holdsworth (London: Ernest Benn, 1974)
H.  William Shakespeare, *Hamlet*, in *The Norton Shakespeare*, ed. Stephen Greenblatt *et al.* (New York: W. W. Norton and Co., 1997)
HKK  Thomas Middleton, *Hengist, King of Kent*, ed. Grace Ioppolo (Oxford: Oxford University Press, 2003)
HW  Thomas Dekker and Thomas Middleton, *The Honest Whore. Part One*, in *The Dramatic Works of Thomas Dekker*, ed. Fredson Bowers, ii (Cambridge: Cambridge University Press, 1950)
KL  William Shakespeare, *King Lear*, in *The Norton Shakespeare*, ed. Stephen Greenblatt *et al.* (New York: W. W. Norton and Co., 1997)
M.  William Shakespeare, *Macbeth*, in *The Norton Shakespeare*, ed. Stephen Greenblatt *et al.* (New York: W. W. Norton and Co., 1997)

| | |
|---|---|
| MT | Thomas Middleton, *Michaelmas Term*, in Middleton, *'A Mad World, My Masters' and Other Plays*, ed. Michael Taylor (Oxford: Oxford University Press, 1995) |
| MWMM | Thomas Middleton, *A Mad World, My Masters*, in Middleton, *'A Mad World, My Masters' and Other Plays*, ed. Michael Taylor (Oxford: Oxford University Press, 1995) |
| OL | Thomas Middleton and William Rowley, *The Old Law*, ed. Catherine M. Shaw (New York: Garland Publishing, 1982) |
| RG | Thomas Middleton, *The Roaring Girl*, ed. Paul Mulholland (Manchester: Manchester University Press, 1987) |
| RL | William Shakespeare, *The Rape of Lucrece*, in *The Norton Shakespeare*, ed. Stephen Greenblatt et al. (New York: W. W. Norton and Co., 1997) |
| RT | Thomas Middleton, *The Revenger's Tragedy*, in Middleton, *Five Plays*, ed. Brian Loughrey and Neil Taylor (London: Penguin, 1988) |
| TA | William Shakespeare, *Timon of Athens*, in *The Norton Shakespeare*, ed. Stephen Greenblatt et al. (New York: W. W. Norton and Co., 1997) |
| TCOO | Thomas Middleton, *A Trick to Catch the Old One*, in Middleton, *Five Plays*, ed. Brian Loughrey and Neil Taylor (London: Penguin, 1988) |
| THI | Thomas Middleton, *The Triumphs of Honour and Industry*, in *The Works of Thomas Middleton*, ed. A .H. Bullen, vii (London: John C. Nimmo, 1886) |
| TI | Thomas Middleton, *The Triumphs of Integrity*, in *The Works of Thomas Middleton*, ed. A.H. Bullen, vii (London: John C. Nimmo, 1886) |
| TT | Thomas Middleton, *The Triumphs of Truth*, in *Jacobean City Pageants*, ed. Richard Dutton (Keele: Keele University Press, 1995) |
| W. | Thomas Middleton, *The Witch*, ed. Elizabeth Schafer (London: A. C. Black, 1994) |
| WBW | Thomas Middleton, *Women Beware Women*, in Middleton, *Five Plays*, ed. Brian Loughrey and Neil Taylor (London: Penguin, 1988) |

# Introduction

In *The Gull's Horn-Book* (1609), a satirical advice-book for gallants, Thomas Dekker describes the playhouse as a

> poets' Royal Exchange, upon which their Muses, that are now turned to merchants, meeting, barter away that light commodity of words for a lighter ware than words – plaudities, and the breath of the great beast; which, like the threatenings of two cowards, vanish all into air. Players are their factors, who put away the stuff, and make the best of it they possibly can, as indeed 'tis their parts so to do.[1]

For Dekker and his contemporaries, as for modern scholars, the theatre is immersed in the marketplace of which it so often speaks. The scene here is not the garret of the romantic imagination, but the playhouse: 'poets' is immediately followed – and redefined – by the Royal Exchange on Threadneedle Street, the commercial heart of London; 'Muses' 'are *now* turned to merchants' – language is a 'light commodity' to 'barter away'. Dekker's words bespeak a world of commerce and exchange, metaphor and simile displacing meaning – an apt conjuring of the economic imperative that governed the playhouse. The 'poets'' hope for 'plaudities' from 'the great beast' (the audience) is dependent on their 'factors', the actors whose 'parts so to do' are literally and metaphorically their role in this economy. There could hardly be a more appropriate way of capturing the material and theatrical realities of playmaking in early modern England.

That the stage was driven by money rather than muse is now a commonplace. Dekker's burlesque is typical of a genre that takes London as its subject, and for a playwright who spent as much of his adult life in debtors' prison as in the theatre his complaint is no doubt sincere as much as satirical. If it chimes with a broader, economically carnivorous world beyond the liberties in which the outdoor playhouses flourished, however, it also registers the stage's internal economy, and in particular a long-neglected feature of playmaking. It is only a slight exaggeration to describe dramatists and actors as 'merchants' and 'factors' (though misleading in class terms), for the raw material of the play script was indeed purchased by players, who fashioned a play for performance before 'the great beast'. This process was, in its linearity, a production line, but it was also a *collaborative* relationship.

When we speak of collaboration, we do so in two ways, both detectable in the passage. The first, most obvious, collaboration is that between playwrights, players and playgoers, who combine to create meaning in the playhouse. On the principle that a play 'happens' only when an audience is present, it is important to recognize the spectators' role in producing theatre. The second meaning neatly combines the commercial and the creative properties of early modern playmaking: collaboration between two or more playwrights commissioned to write a playscript. As will become apparent, this form of composition encompasses several categories, including revising, adding to and reworking a text, with or without the original writer(s); indeed, it is only now becoming clear how an understanding of collaboration can inform our knowledge of early modern drama.

This book is centrally concerned with a major playwright, Thomas Middleton, and the conjunction joining him to a number of collaborators. The *and* in the title is not a mere syntactical detail. Despite G. E. Bentley's calculation that Philip Henslowe's account book of plays staged at the Rose playhouse in the decade to 1604 indicates that, of 282, nearly two-thirds were written by more than one writer,[2] collaboration has received scant attention. Middleton is also less prominent than he deserves. This study draws on current theories of collaboration in its examination of Thomas Middleton. He is perhaps the ideal candidate: of the major dramatists, only Marlowe (who was dead) and Chapman do not feature in Middleton's career. His most highly regarded plays are, fittingly, both sole efforts realized in collaboration with actors and audiences, and collaborations with other playwrights.

# INTRODUCTION

Middleton appears to have left Oxford without taking a degree and followed the path of numerous others attracted to London, whose population rose rapidly in the century after 1550. Like other educated young men, he was drawn to playhouses, and in 1601 is recorded as 'daylie accompanynge the players'. Over the next twenty years he was to write, or contribute to, poems, plays, city pageants and entertainments, and pamphlets, many of which directly or allegorically evoke contemporary London. Although championed by influential critics such as Gary Taylor as a radical alternative to Shakespeare,[3] Middleton largely remains, in the words of T. S. Eliot, 'merely the name one associates with six or seven great plays'.[4] An unmistakably *political* Middleton has since emerged, however, and his Protestant opposition to King James's overtures to Spain, culminating in the remarkable *A Game at Chess*, is well established.[5] Yet Eliot's judgement that he 'collaborated shamelessly'[6] has helped perpetuate the notion that collaborative writing is a lesser form of art, despite Eliot's own recognition that one collaboration, *The Changeling* (1622), 'stands above every tragic play of its time, except those of Shakespeare'.[7]

All early modern dramatists are measured against Shakespeare, but Middleton's proximity to him is greater than most. Their professional relationship is one of the most intriguing issues, with important implications for how each is regarded, separately and together. Crucially, it is when the question of possible collaboration arises that a more accurate picture of early modern playmaking emerges. Like many of his peers, Middleton got his start by joining a small group of dramatists, contributing a scene or plot here and there; like many of his contemporaries, he was to continue in this vein throughout his career. What we now know about playmaking reveals not only that 'collaboration was the standard mode of operation within the early modern English theater',[8] but that it produced great drama. It is timely, then, to focus on collaboration, not only as a material fact but for what it might tell us about the composition, performance and reception of plays that, as Dekker pithily observes, 'vanish all into air'.

The present study draws on recent theoretical perspectives to inform its approach to the professional careers of dramatists for whom 'muse' and 'merchant' were often perhaps uneasy but equally demanding bedfellows. The previous book on Middleton in this series was published in 1979: it is a sign of changing perspectives that a study of Middleton is now, necessarily, also a study of collaboration. As editors and scholars appreciate, Middleton's career resists easy classification. He wrote for the children's companies in the early years of the seventeenth century, contributed plays designed for both outdoor and indoor theatres, and worked both as a 'freelance' writer with good connections and as a dramatist closely associated with the King's Men. He is one of the chief exponents of 'city' or 'citizen' comedy,[9] yet he also wrote tragedies and tragicomedies. That his writing relations are difficult to map other than by way of a chronology is a further reminder that dramatists wrote essentially to commission. Middleton is important to theatre historians partly because he had a finger in so many pies.

The layout of this book is correspondingly thematic rather than chronological. We begin with a chapter on Middleton *solus*, which serves, it is hoped, as an account of his career onto which subsequent discussions may be mapped. Chapter 2 fleshes out some of the issues surrounding collaboration and traces Middleton's relations with his fellow playwrights. Three of these, those with whom he most frequently associated, are given chapters of their own, the readings of his collaborative work with Dekker, Shakespeare and Rowley exploring issues and possibilities sketched out earlier. Finally, the touchstone of the study, collaboration, is applied to Middleton alone. If he was comfortable working with other playwrights, it is not surprising that he repeatedly returned to his own plays (as well as those of others) to echo, rework and refashion images and ideas, verbal and visual, for 'judicious spectators'.[10] His career was, in myriad ways, one long collaboration.

# 1

# Middleton

This chapter will examine what is generally regarded as the unaided work of Thomas Middleton. The main focus will be on his dramatic output. The plays participate in debates on current social and political concerns: shifting viewpoints, re-presentation of themes, rewriting of dramatic situations in different genres, and a characteristic mixing of genres suggest a writer who looks at contemporary ideas and issues from a range of perspectives in an attempt to come to terms with a changing world. These features make Thomas Middleton a writer who is recognizably very modern.

Most of Middleton's life was spent in London, and experience of the city informs much of his work. Indeed, he has been called 'a key voice of London... in the first quarter of the seventeenth-century'.[1] London provides one of two points of focus in this chapter. The other is the world of the court, increasingly the setting for plays after about 1613, and an indication of a growing engagement in political debate at a time when he was writing pageants and entertainments for city employers.

## 'A KEY VOICE OF LONDON'

The London about which Middleton was writing in the early years of the seventeenth century was undergoing considerable expansion. Large-scale migration from the countryside brought changes in social relations. The majority of worker migrants were single and had left family units in other parts of the country, thus fracturing family ties. They came to an unfamiliar environment, lacking the identity and support provided by a family in a small rural community. Crowded and unsanitary living conditions led to frequent outbreaks of plague and high mortality rates. Despite this, the continuing influx led to a significant increase in London's population. One of the effects of high mortality was to make remarriage after a short interval very common in order to maintain a family or household, simply as a matter of survival.[2] A widower with children would need someone to look after them while he worked, whilst a widow would often be in need of male protection and economic support. Prostitution might be the only recourse for a woman left to fend for herself. The upper classes had always used marriage for economic and social benefit, as well as dynastic advancement, but the problem of survival in the city, particularly for migrants, meant that for the lower classes too economic forces often assumed a greater importance in marriage than personal emotions. Middleton's earliest non-dramatic writings include satires with contemporary London as their focus: *Microcynicon: Six Snarling Satires* (1599) in verse, and *The Black Book* (1604) and *Father Hubbard's Tales* (1604) in prose. These works display a concern for the working poor and the disadvantaged, and criticism of the greed and idleness of the rich. The effects of social and economic factors on matters of identity and personal relationships feature prominently in Middleton's city comedies, and more widely in his works, showing a world at a crucial point of change from medieval to modern, when long-held values and assumptions about human nature, gender, society and its institutions were being challenged.

The early comedy *The Phoenix* (1604), though set in Ferrara, contains material similar to Middleton's comedies of London life. The plots involving the litigious man, Tangle, and the corrupt justice, Falso, with their satire on the law, and the plots of the Jeweller's Wife who pursues an adulterous affair with the Knight, and the Captain who sells his wife, with their focus on marriage and sexual exchange, would not be out of place in those comedies. However, the inclusion of a ruler figure, the court setting of the first and last scenes, and the plot to assassinate the Duke and his son, are not characteristic of the genre, but rather point forward to *The Revenger's Tragedy* (1606) and even to a much later play, *Women Beware Women* (c.1621). Indeed, *The Phoenix*'s schematic structure also sets it apart from the other city comedies: Tangle is contrasted to Quieto, the peaceful man; set speeches on marriage and on law formally set out in the early scenes ideals against which the corruptions of the dukedom are defined; characters are chosen to represent specific institutions and classes, giving a broad perspective of the body politic. The various plot strands are held together by the authority figure, Prince Phoenix, who goes about incognito to spy out abuses, and who acts as supreme judge in the concluding scene. Here Middleton draws on the dramatic convention of the disguised ruler, which Shakespeare used in *Measure for Measure*, written in the same year. Middleton was to use the convention again in a slightly different form in a collaborative play, *The Old Law* (1618), and also revised Shakespeare's play in 1621.[3] None of Middleton's other comedies of London life conveys the impression of such simple control or such clear-cut issues as *The Phoenix*.

Of the comedies written between 1604 and 1606, *Michaelmas Term* provides a striking contrast in its presentation of the city. An allegorical Induction, an unusual feature in Middleton's city comedies, establishes as the powerful controller of this world not a reforming prince but the personification of Michaelmas Term, the main term of the legal year when people poured into London on a flood of litigation. Middleton presents him as a gigantic figure of gargantuan appetite, who grasps almost the entire proceeds of the country harvest in his 'contentious fathom' (*MT*, Induction 9). He presents London as a type of hell, and the infernal image continues throughout the play. Michaelmas Term's appetite for clients is insatiable, and the throngs of people suggest not only litigants but the migrants flocking to London. Michaelmas Term is, in many respects, a personification of London itself, described later in the play as 'this man-devouring city' (*MT* II. ii. 21), and Quomodo, its chief representative, as 'a most merciless devourer' (*MT* III. iv. 74). The city reduces its inhabitants to consumable flesh. Hellgill's words, as he tries to procure the Country Wench by telling her how rich men will seek her favours if she turns courtesan – 'The gilded flies will light upon thy flesh' (*MT* I. ii. 46) – reduce the girl to a piece of meat. This idea is given more striking currency later in *A Chaste Maid in Cheapside* (1613), where another Country Wench, with an illegitimate baby, gets the better of two corrupt agents of the city government who are supposed to enforce regulations against the eating of meat in Lent (*CMC* II. ii). She leads them to believe her baby, hidden in a basket, is a joint of meat, and when they take it from her they are left literally holding the baby. The scene provides a striking *gestus* of the city's power to turn persons into consumable commodities. Behind the descriptions of London as infernal, voracious devourer lie vestigial suggestions of the hell-mouth of medieval drama that consumed the damned. The mention of prostitutes by Michaelmas Term in the Induction, developed later in the Country Wench's transformation into a courtesan, might remind spectators that the city was traditionally gendered as female, and therefore the 'man-devouring city' might itself be represented as the prostitute, with her genitalia, Lear's 'sulphurous pit' (*KL* IV. v. 122), providing a secular equivalent to the religious hell-mouth.

As Michael Taylor observes, 'There is a whiff of sulphur in the air of most of Middleton's city comedies'.[4] In *A Mad World, My Masters*, the devil as succubus is actually presented on stage to tempt Penitent Brothel (*MWMM* IV. i. 29). Witgood in *A Trick to Catch the Old One*, pursued by his creditors, feels he is in hell pursued by devils (*TCOO* IV. iii. 58–9), and, in the same play, Dampit is linked not only nominally with hell, but described as 'like the devil in chains' (*TCOO* IV. v. 6). Michael Hattaway observes that such references to devils after the sixteenth century provide 'metaphors for the uncontrollable forces of the city economy'.[5] *A Chaste Maid in Cheapside* clearly shows economic forces undermining religion, and in turn social institutions. The play is set in the Christian penitential season of Lent, a time of fasting and religious discipline. The irony is that the city is shown as a place of indulgence and indiscipline, with a disorderly and indulgent christening scene providing a prime example of dissolution. Later in the play the young lovers, Moll and Touchwood Junior, are reported to be dead and given a joint funeral, at which, when everyone present expresses the wish that they could have been married, they rise up out of their coffins. It is a resurrection scene, an appropriate conclusion to a play set in Lent, the season that ends with the Easter celebration of Jesus's resurrection. The pursuit of desire in the city is set against the religious framework of the play with ironic effect, providing a sense of serious dislocation between the way people actually live and the values upon which societal institutions are based.

The city's power of transformation, in terms not only of commodification but also of identity, is a major concern in the city comedies. Instability of identity is emphasized by the frequent uses of disguise and assumed roles, such as the Courtesan as Widow Medlar in *A Trick to Catch the Old One* or Follywit as Lord Owemuch in *A Mad World, My Masters*, but none deals so fully and inventively with it as *No Wit, No Help like a Woman's* (1611). Characters adopt disguises in this play, but its most striking feature is the way in which the question of Grace's identity is handled. Before the play opens, Lady Twilight and her daughter, Grace, have been abducted by privateers while on a sea voyage. Philip Twilight goes in search of his mother and sister, taking ransom money for them, but, while he is abroad, he falls in love with, and marries, a young woman, spending the ransom to bring her home. He pretends she is his sister and his mother is dead, but Lady Twilight returns, and Philip is persuaded to confess to her. She forgives him and is prepared to pretend that Grace is her daughter to protect her son from his father's wrath, until she hears from Grace that she was sold by privateers; convinced that she really is her daughter, she believes Philip has committed incest. The problem of Grace's identity is resolved by a device from romance rather than satirical comedy: in the final scene Lady Goldenfleece reveals that, when Grace was a baby, her nurse changed her own child for the Twilights' daughter, and so Grace is not Philip's sister after all.

*No Wit, No Help like a Woman's* shows the satiric edge of city comedy softened by romance. The play has the usual references to specific London locations, and the parallel plot of Mistress Low-water and Lady Goldenfleece takes the familiar city comedy theme of money or property returned through a trick to its rightful owner. However, lost parents, pirates and child-swapping do not depend upon a London setting at all. Unstable and shifting identity, though a prominent city comedy theme, is not here an almost inevitable result of the city's powers of metamorphosis, or of its many deceptions, or its characterization as a place of mists, as in *Your Five Gallants* (1607). Rather, the twists and turns of the plot with regard to Grace's identity occur from chance events. *No Wit, No Help like a Woman's* is a transitional play between Middleton's city comedies and the tragicomedies written in the second decade of the century. Though sharing generic properties, Middleton's city comedies individually show shifts in perspective on living in an emerging capitalist society. Examination of changes and differences within the group provides insights into questions addressed in other Middleton plays. In *The Phoenix* the presence of a presiding authority figure is linked with a dominant concern about control of subversive and disorderly forces. In *Michaelmas Term* we see a reverse picture of the city, in which the presiding authority is the eponymous, immoral figure. However, although this play too ends with a judgment scene, in the law court, there is ambiguity: if Easy and Thomasine are like the young lovers of other comedies, they do not win through to marriage in the end. Moreover, there is considerable ambiguity in Thomasine's line about the judge – 'he knows me well' (*MT* V. i. 124). Here is an acknowledgement of complexities that render impossible the simple control system and solutions of *The Phoenix*.

*A Trick to Catch the Old One* and *A Mad World, My Masters* lack formal judgment scenes and presiding authority figures. In these plays the amoral trickster figure is foregrounded. In the Hobbesian 'war of every man against every man', or at least of citizens against gentry, which Quomodo identifies as the condition of society in *Michaelmas Term* (*MT* I. i. 108–9), it is a matter of the survival of the wittiest. Precisely because those who hold power are themselves tricksters, and their deceptions create an uncertain and hostile environment, it is necessary for others to become tricksters to survive. Initiative and quickness of mind, the ability to solve problems by lateral thinking, rather than by conscience, are the qualities most valued in this world, and they were precisely the qualities needed for success in the emerging capitalist system.

So where do the plays position the audience in relation to these matters? In some places the activities of tricksters appear to be condemned as undermining the religious foundation of societal institutions, yet in other places trickery is endorsed. William R. Dynes distinguishes a continuum from altruistic to egocentric tricksters in Jacobean city comedies.[6] Witgood in *A*

*Trick to Catch the Old One* and Follywit in *A Mad World, My Masters* both have names that highlight the importance of wit to the recovery of their fortunes, but they are treated differently: Follywit is more of an egocentric trickster whereas Witgood not only regains his lands, but also provides a husband for his former mistress, thus suggesting a combination of egocentric and altruistic. Follywit, though given money by his uncle, endures the double embarrassment of being caught out with the watch he has stolen from him, and of discovering that the woman he has married was his uncle's mistress. The shifting nature of viewpoints in these city comedies suggests debate about important issues in a changing society. Although the tricksters of city comedies may trace their lineage back to the witty and ingenious slave of Roman New Comedy who solves his master's problems, or is instrumental in bringing matters to a happy conclusion, the trickster figure itself has a more ancient lineage reaching back to the mythologies of early societies worldwide. He serves many functions: he may, for instance, be a weak and vulnerable animal who outwits a more powerful predator, and therefore potentially expresses popular feeling against authority. The way he outwits others may involve ingenious and unconventional ideas, so that he solves problems by his ability to adopt a mindset different from those around him. In a society undergoing fundamental change, the foregrounding of this figure signals the need to approach new problems from new perspectives: in dealing with the problems created by an emerging capitalist society, there can be no going back to the traditional ways of a previous age.

Later Middleton city comedies juxtapose one perspective to another. In *A Chaste Maid in Cheapside* the plot involving Allwit has a satirical perspective in which Allwit is condemned for moral laxity in allowing Whorehound to get his children for him, while, on the other hand, the plot of the Kixes, in which Touchwood Senior fathers their children, involves no such condemnation, but rather a festive satisfaction that their individual problems of barrenness and excessive fertility are resolved in such a mutual fashion. In *No Wit, No Help Like a Woman's*, the two plots present alternative perspectives: the one involving Mistress Low-water places an emphasis on the importance of personal initiative and action in solving problems, as in earlier city comedies, while, on the other hand, the Twilights' plot shows problems solved not by personal action but by factors over which the characters have no control. Here we find evidence of debate about the scope for individual action to bring about change and to determine the course of events, set against a sense of living in a society where there is an increasing awareness that human lives are affected by large-scale social and economic forces over which the individual has no control.

The seven pageants for the inauguration of Lord Mayors, and the civic entertainments Middleton was commissioned to write for city companies from 1613 onwards, address the matter of urban living from another angle. Quomodo in *Michaelmas Term* had identified the city as a site of social warfare between citizens and gentry, but official commissions required a change of perspective, and this is reflected in the presentation of London in the first, and finest, of the pageants, *The Triumphs of Truth*, written for the inauguration of the writer's namesake, Sir Thomas Middleton of the Grocers' Company, in 1613. At the opening the city's inhabitants are presented as members of a family: London is a mother, greeting her son, the new Lord Mayor. Later, fraternal themes are emphasized as, at the Triumphant Mount, Perfect Love holds the Sphere of Brotherhood bearing the arms of the twelve companies. London's opening speech emphasizes reciprocal gifts and responsibilities: as a loving mother she has brought up Sir Thomas, and now, in age, she submits herself to his care. This is a very different view of London from that projected in the city comedies, where the representative figures are the female prostitute and the rapacious male entrepreneur. However, we should not assume that Middleton abandons his probing vision of the problems of life in the expanding city for an idealistic perspective in a craven attempt to please his new employers. There is a recognition here, and in other city pageants of the period, that for many of London's new immigrants familial ties had been fractured and their sense of belonging to a community lost, as a result of which a new kind of *communitas* needed to be developed, and that the individualistic and competitive energies, which the expanding city encouraged, needed to be harnessed for the benefit of the community. In rural communities lives were given shape and meaning with the seasons and seasonal activities, like harvest time. The annual mayoral inauguration pageant on 29 October, with its sense of completion and renewal, provided an important secular point of reference when the urban community came together, giving shape to the urban year.

Though the pageants could be viewed as no more than cynical attempts by worried city authorities to defuse potential disorder by laying an emphasis on sharing and reciprocity, alternatively they could be seen as proposing new ways in which stable identity and a sense of connection and relationship might be established. The rich and successful in city government are urged in the pageants to use their power and wealth for works of charity and benevolence, to have, as *The Triumphs of Honour and Industry* (1617) puts it, 'a virtuous care | Of the oppressed' (*THI* 304). The expressions of concern for the poor and the powerless throughout Middleton's work suggest that these words are likely to have been genuinely felt rather than being merely a pious attempt to please his new employers.

At the beginning of *The Triumphs of Truth* London implies that Sir Thomas Middleton has reached his eminent position through desert, and the theme of honour related to works or merit, rather than to birth or riches, is one that recurs in Middleton's pageants. The city concept of honour and the importance of an active life of self-improvement is expressed in *The Triumphs of Integrity* (1623), where the new Lord Mayor, Sir Martin Lumley, is praised for having risen from humble origins (*TI* 387). The annual change of mayor showed that it was theoretically possible for any member of the urban community to reach high office, thus appealing to the new spirit of aspiration. However, having reached the mayoralty, the successful man has no easy life: in *The Triumphs of Truth* Mother London warns him of the many trials and temptations he will face during his year of office, and the reappearance of the mists of Error at a number of points during the pageant remind spectators that he will need continual vigilance to counter challenges to his and the city's integrity. Indeed, these may come from inside the city itself. Though London is presented as a mother, implying that the citizens are her children, the pageant does not present the city family as harmonious and united, for she acknowledges that she has other sons, the opposites of Sir Thomas, 'thankless, unkind, and disobedient' (*TT* 145). James Knowles emphasizes that inter-guild relations were complex and marked by competition and disputes.[7] The stress on virtuous action rather than birth in the mayoral pageants sets city government in contrast to the court, but *The Triumphs of Truth* does not present a polarization between the two because many great merchants of the city, like Sir Thomas Middleton, had close business dealings with courtiers. The merchants needed government to sanction privileged trading companies and to prevent foreign competition. They served on most royal commissions concerning trade, and were thus drawn into closer contact and collaboration with the Crown. The pressures for cooperation between the merchant community and the Crown were increasing in the early seventeenth century.[8] However, just as the city was not a unified family, the Jacobean court was a site of conflicting interests. There is evidence to suggest that *The Triumphs of Truth* was an intervention in City politics, and expressed a view critical of associations of the city with Robert Carr, the King's favourite, and with the Howard faction at court.[9] It is with *The Triumphs of Truth* that Middleton's work appears to become increasingly political, and the city pageants provide an interface between two key subjects within it, London and the court.

## COURT WORLDS: 'IT'S A WITTY AGE'

Gendering the city as female, as a figure of submission to patriarchy, might have been seen by James I as an appropriate acknowledgement of the nature of the political relationship of City to Crown.[10] However, despite his presentation of Mother London in *The Triumphs of Truth*, there is little evidence in Middleton's work of flattery of those in power. He does express hope in Prince Charles as the next ruler in the idealized White Knight in *A Game at Chess* (1624), and at moments in *The World Tossed at Tennis* (1620, with Rowley) and in *The Triumphs of Integrity*, the latter pageant containing compliments to the King. However, the White King in *A Game at Chess* and Constantius in *Hengist, King of Kent* (1620), aspects of whom might have suggested James I to an audience, could hardly have been regarded as flattering. For the most part, courts and rulers in Middleton's plays are presented critically.

There seems little doubt that the critical view of the Italian courts in Jacobean tragedy and tragi-comedy was a reflection on the court of King James. With the death in 1612 of James's closest adviser, Robert Cecil, who had been minister to Queen Elizabeth, power increasingly fell into the hands of royal favourites, first Robert Carr, Viscount Rochester, later Earl of Somerset, and then George Villiers, Marquis, later Duke, of Buckingham. The best way of access to the King was through the favourite, and suitors might have to make a number of payments to several intermediaries before their suit could reach him. Hand in hand with bribery went sycophancy. Middleton's *The Revenger's Tragedy* presents a decadent court. A series of highly descriptive speeches in the first six scenes of the play establishes a world of lust, gluttony, drunkenness and all manner of excess. Though this is a court world, there are clear connections with the world of Middleton's city comedies: the play's satiric exuberance, sardonic wit and a series of superbly theatrical ironic reversals bring it close to comedy – even, at times, to farce. The protagonist, Vindice, in pursuing revenge against the Duke for the murder of Gloriana, is a trickster figure. He kills the Duke by a witty contrivance, poisoning him with Gloriana's skull painted to resemble a courtesan in a darkened summerhouse. The revenger as witty trickster is acknowledged in the latter part of the play: 'Thus much by wit a deep revenger can, | When murder's known to be the clearest man' (*RT* V. i. 85–6); ''twas somewhat wittily carried' (*RT* V. iii. 96). This last statement comes when Vindice boasts to Antonio about his revenge. In tragedy the trickster is usually a villain: Guardiano, in *Women Beware Women*, comments with satisfaction as he recalls how he brought the unwitting Bianca to her violation in Livia's picture gallery – 'it's a witty age' (*WBW* II. ii. 398) – signalling his relation to other ingenious contrivers in Middleton's plays. *The Revenger's Tragedy*'s frequent ironic reversals suggest that there is no certainty in this court world, where kin relationships dissolve under pressure of material considerations, and gold, as in the city comedies, works its transformations.

   The depiction of court life and sensational action in *The Revenger's Tragedy* does not directly refer to the Jacobean court, but carries a general emotional charge and critical vision that may express responses to it in the early years of the reign. Ten years on, life began to imitate art with a number of sensational scandals that made the Italianate courts of Jacobean tragedy seem less far removed from the English court. Foremost of these were the Essex divorce, the poisoning of Sir Thomas Overbury in the Tower of London, and the subsequent trials and conviction for murder of the King's favourite, Robert Carr, Earl of Somerset, and his wife, Frances Howard. The daughter of the Earl of Suffolk, she had been married at the age of 13 to the 14-year-old Earl of Essex. In 1612 Carr fell in love with Frances Howard; the King was sympathetic, and set up a divorce commission. At the hearing Frances Howard claimed that her marriage had been unconsummated as her husband had been bewitched, resulting in his impotence. This was the first of a number of references to witchcraft in these court scandals. Frances Howard was widely believed to have committed adultery with Carr, but the King packed the Divorce Commission to obtain the desired annulment in her favour, thus, in the eyes of many, assisting vice, and undermining justice and religion. Carr's closest friend and adviser, Sir Thomas Overbury, had tried to persuade him against marriage to the Countess to stop him becoming involved with the Howard faction, who then managed to have him imprisoned in the Tower, where he was later poisoned. Carr and Frances Howard were accused of his murder, their accomplices tried and executed, and they themselves found guilty. The King showed mercy and commuted the death penalty to imprisonment in the Tower, from which they were released in 1622. The murder trials led to sensational revelations not only of poisoning but of witchcraft amid strong rumours of a Catholic plot. At the trials, Lord Chief Justice Coke hinted repeatedly that the investigation of the murder of Overbury had uncovered a popish plot, which he likened to the Gunpowder Plot of 1605.[11] These matters were the subject of much talk and speculation, and of many scurrilous verses, and newsheets.

    Court factional politics played a large part in these crises. The Howards wanted a marriage alliance with Carr, particularly as he had hitherto sided with the strongly Protestant group at court, which then attempted to put forward a rival favourite, George Villiers. With the fall of Carr, Villiers's rise was assured. These court divisions were also related to responses to the King's foreign policy, in particular his pacific stance towards

Catholic Spain, his later failure to assist his Protestant son-in-law, the Elector Palatine, when his territories were attacked by Catholic forces in 1619–20, and his attempts to arrange a marriage between Prince Charles and the Spanish infanta – matters at the heart of Middleton's political satire *A Game at Chess*.

As there is evidence to suggest that *The Triumphs of Truth* was an intervention in the politics of the City, critical of the City's connections with Robert Carr, so critics have also identified political material and topical allusions in the plays that followed. Alastair Bellany has suggested that, in popular writing at the time of the Overbury murder trials, the subjects of witchcraft, gender disorder, sexual transgression, syphilitic infection, use of cosmetics and poison all had political connotations, particularly linked to fears of foreign, and especially Catholic, corruption.[12] His findings provide insights into how plays dealing with such matters at this particular time might have been understood by their audiences. Whereas *The Revenger's Tragedy* engages in generalized satire of court worlds, after about 1613 Middleton's targets are more specific. His plays with court, or quasi-court, settings may be loosely divided into two groups: one comprises *The Lady's Tragedy* (1611), *More Dissemblers Besides Women* (1614), *Hengist, King of Kent* and *A Game at Chess*; the other *The Witch* (c.1616) and *Women Beware Women*.

The first group dwells less upon aristocratic corruption than attempts to undermine ideals of chaste and faithful womanhood. Protestant discourse frequently employed the figures of the pure woman and the whore to represent Protestantism and Catholicism, and it may be that these plays deal rather more with concerns about confessional conflict than with court corruption, though there is some overlap. *The Witch* and *Women Beware Women* are related to *The Revenger's Tragedy* by their emphasis on corrupt courts, but more particularly these later plays appear to make significant reference to specific persons and events, especially the scandals surrounding Carr and Howard, and the matter of the favourite. Overlap between the groups occurs, however, as *The Lady's Tragedy* and *Hengist, King of Kent* both contain references to Frances Howard.[13] We should not expect a strict separation between the topics of confessional conflict and court corruption, as they were connected through the Howards' pro-Catholic stance, belief that courtiers and particularly court ladies were in the pay of Spain, and rumours that the murder of Overbury was linked to a Catholic plot. Though the first group of plays is generically mixed – *The Lady's Tragedy* is a tragedy, *More Dissemblers Besides Women* a tragicomedy, *Hengist, King of Kent* a chronicle history with elements of tragicomedy and city comedy, and *Game* a political satire – there are interesting connections between them. Early in his career Middleton had treated the subject of the violation of the chaste ideal in his poem *The Ghost of Lucrece* (1600). In *The Lady's Tragedy*, the Lady is courted by the lustful Tyrant, and commits suicide, like Lucrece. Anne Lancashire argues that the main plot may intermittently allow of an allegorical moral and religious interpretation concerned with the conflict between Protestantism and Catholicism.[14] She even suggests the possibility that it may focus on the court of James I as a site of that conflict, presenting 'an allegory of Roman Catholicism . . . attempting to turn the true Church (the Lady), daughter of Protestantism (Helvetius) . . . into the Roman Catholic Church'.[15] If this is so, it would link the play with *Hengist, King of Kent*, where application to contemporary religio-political concerns is more obvious: Castiza, whose name indicates purity, betrothed to the murdered king, Constantius, is forced to marry the usurper, Vortiger, but he is seduced by the pagan princess, Roxena, as part of the Saxon invaders' plot to take over Britain. Vortiger falsely accuses Castiza of impurity so that he can marry Roxena. Reflecting the symbolic figures of the pure woman and the whore from Protestant discourse, Castiza and Roxena signify pure and false religion. The play expresses concern that James I was coming under Catholic influence, and that he was intending to marry his heir to the Spanish infanta.[16]

*A Game at Chess* is allegorical and overtly political. It brings such matters into sharper focus, leaving little doubt about interpretation. The action takes place on a chess board, with the white pieces representing England and the black pieces Spain. The Black Bishop's Pawn's attempt to seduce the White Queen's Pawn has been seen as an allegory of the attempt to subvert the Church of England. Such an interpretation strengthens the case for political readings of other narratives of the defamation of chaste women in Middleton's work. In *More Dissemblers Besides*

*Women* the central character, the Duchess of Milan, who has vowed to her late husband never to remarry, shows her constancy when the Cardinal, who has praised her as an example to all women, encourages her to remarry from motives of self-interest. The matter of constancy, the emphasis on vows and the leading role played by the Cardinal, suggest a concern here with religion; while the historical material in *Hengist, King of Kent* and the overt political allegory of *A Game at Chess* make it possible to identify plausible references to contemporary religio-political matters, the tragicomic material of *More Dissemblers Besides Women* is more opaque. Nevertheless, given Middleton's interventions in contemporary debates and responses to current events, it is likely that *More Dissemblers Besides Women* also dealt with such matters, and that a Jacobean audience would have been alert to them.

*The Witch* and *Women Beware Women* deal rather more with corruption and the scandalous nature of court life. Although there is no conclusive evidence for an exact date for *The Witch*, which was not published until 1778, it appears to refer extensively to the Essex divorce and Overbury murder trials. When the murder came to light, Frances Howard was vilified as a witch, so the play's title might well have indicated the possibility of topical readings, as would the naming of a character Francisca (that is, Frances Carr). A number of intersections between the play and the scandal have been noted,[17] and the fact that courtiers get away with plotting murder and no one is punished for using the witches' services might have suggested parallels with the outcome of the trial of Frances Howard.

Both *The Witch* and *Women Beware Women* present worlds of distorted values or hypocrisy, and both have as a central concern the institution of marriage. *The Witch* opens with a marriage feast that is an orgy of drunkenness and gluttony, and the bridegroom reveals he will keep a mistress. At the end of the play the Duke thanks heaven for his wife, because, although the Duchess planned to have him murdered, she did not commit adultery. Similarly, in *Women Beware Women* the Duke responds apparently with repentance to the Cardinal's condemnation of his adulterous relationship with Bianca by vowing that he will never keep woman 'unlawfully' (*WBW* IV. i. 254) again, and keeps to the letter of his vow by seeing to it that her husband, Leantio, is killed, so that Bianca is free to marry him. Livia, the play's arch manipulator, covers her machinations with expressions of concern for others: she says she is 'pitiful' towards Hippolito for his incestuous passion for his niece, Isabella, and is determined to help him (*WBW* II. i. 41). Later, the Duke, attempting to seduce Bianca, tells her he pitied her for her lack of comforts in Leantio's house (*WBW* II. ii. 380). These instances of false or misplaced pity draw attention to the moral distortions of the court world.

*The Witch* lacks the clarity of narrative (there are four plots) and the technical assurance of *The Revenger's Tragedy*. By contrast the design of *Women Beware Women* makes it the supreme achievement among his solo works. No other Jacobean tragedy stresses so clearly how social and economic forces shape and change people's lives. The opening of the play in the house of a humble citizen rather than in a court might suggest a comedy of urban life: although it is ostensibly set in Medicean Florence, many details suggest Jacobean London. Indeed, Middleton takes his analysis much further than in his earlier comedies, widening his scrutiny to reveal how social and economic forces are related to the actions of those who hold power. The dramatist shows how the corruption and cynicism of an idle and pleasure-loving court contaminate the lives of ordinary, hard-working citizens. In this he shows a concern for the powerless and poor found in earlier works. The opening scene stresses social and economic factors through the reactions of the Mother to Leantio's revelation that he has married a Venetian heiress and brought her home. Her words of concern about Bianca's ability to be happy in their humble household are paralleled later by the Duke's persuasion of Bianca to become his mistress: he can offer her a comfortable life free from want. Leantio describes Bianca as a jewel, which he has stolen (*WBW* I. i. 162). His awareness she must be locked away, as he lives in an acquisitive society, proves to be well founded when Bianca is stolen by the greatest thief of all, the ruler.

Bianca is procured for the Duke by Livia, who flatters the Mother, a part-time serving woman in her house, by treating her as if they were social equals, inviting her to keep her company and play chess, while Bianca is shown round the house by

Guardiano. The audience is made aware of the polite social veneer concealing predatory motives. Guardiano shows Bianca fine paintings ostensibly as a gesture of consideration and hospitality to a stranger, but actually with the intention of using the 'naked pictures' (*WBW* II. ii. 405) as pornographic preparation for the Duke's assault. The use of art as pornography and the rape of Bianca that occurs in a picture gallery might well have carried a particular charge at a time when courtiers, and particularly the royal favourites Carr and Villiers, were building up art collections to express their magnificence and power.

The use of art as an expression of power was to be found most clearly in the Jacobean and Caroline periods in the masques performed at court, in which courtiers, and even the queen, might appear in the guise of gods, goddesses, heroes, and other mythological characters. These lavish entertainments were a means of promoting court ideology. The final scene of *Women Beware Women* presents a masque for the celebration of Bianca's marriage to the Duke that becomes an expression not of courtly ideals but of courtly rivalries. The tone of much of this final scene is one of mockery mixed with horror, as bizarre deaths and misunderstandings occur with considerable rapidity. A double perspective on the court is presented: the scene is a prime example of 'horrid laughter',[18] evoking both horror at the carnage and a sense of absurdity that these persons should bring about their own destruction in pursuit of the fulfilment of their desires.

In *Women Beware Women* a number of current concerns find a focus. Zara Bruzzi finds reference to Frances Howard through echoes of masques for her marriages to Essex and Carr in the play, and also argues that it deals with the matter of the favourite, suggesting both Somerset and Buckingham.[19] The title also draws attention to debates about women, which had been fuelled by Joseph Swetnam's *The Arraignment of Lewd, Idle, Froward, and Unconstant Women* (1615), the various ripostes it elicited, and interest in the scandal of Frances Howard. *Women Beware Women*, like the city comedies, presents the commodification of women by men. Both Isabella and Bianca become hard and calculating characters, but the play may be read as suggesting that patriarchal attitudes have made them so, and, in the case of Bianca, we might regard her as adopting survival techniques. A stranger in the city, with no one to turn to if her possessive husband finds out what has happened, she accepts the security of being the ruler's mistress rather than being a common prostitute.

The double plot structure sets up contrasts between a marriage based on mutual attraction, which defies society's rules, and an upper-class arranged marriage, which raises questions about women's freedom of choice. In the second scene Livia speaks up for Isabella, telling Fabritio that his daughter ought at least to be consulted about her proposed husband – sentiments a present-day audience might feel should be taken as providing a statement of acceptable values in the play. However, the play soon subverts audience expectations as Livia becomes a cunning manipulator and underminer of marriage, working in the interests of men. Livia is not a woman who has been conditioned to accept patriarchy without giving it a thought, she is too independently minded for that; but she does see that her own interests are best advanced in a patriarchal society by providing the Duke with what he wants.

Though the religious perspective of Middleton's writings has been recognized as Calvinist,[20] and the political perspective as that of someone who opposed the Spanish marriage, supported the call for military assistance in the Palatinate, and adopted a stance on the home front that was generally critical of Carr and Buckingham, it is much more difficult to define precisely where the plays stand in relation to debates about women. The title, *Women Beware Women*, seems to suggest an anti-women stance, but *More Dissemblers Besides Women* suggests an opposite view – beware men too! The plays themselves are more complex than their titles might suggest. They participate in the debate, encouraging audiences to think about the issues. This is a characteristic of Middleton plays at their best, such as *A Chaste Maid in Cheapside*, where the complexity of the plotting introduces so many comparative perspectives. The audience of a Middleton play is continually shocked out of its complacency, disoriented, as it assumes a question has been answered, a perspective provided or a reliable commentator identified, only to be shown alternatives.

Shock, disorientation and a process of reassessment are to be found in the final act of *Women Beware Women*. The play suddenly changes from one that has conveyed a sense of life as it was really lived in the houses of poor citizens and courtiers, with many domestic details contributing to our sense of that reality, to one that presents in this court scene absurd and confused events, creating a sense of unreality and insanity as the courtiers use the masque as a cover for their elaborate acts of revenge. Tragic and almost farcical elements combine, as one bizarre death rapidly follows another, creating confusion both for the audience in the theatre and for the stage audience, as the Duke puzzles over the discrepancy between his synopsis and what he is witnessing. The radical dramaturgy that brings about this change in the last act produces an apocalyptic vision, as Irving Ribner has suggested, of an entire society in collapse; indeed, he describes the play as 'a dramatic symbol of the damnation of all mankind'.[21] The inclination of the audience may be to laugh at the events of Act V as incredible, yet at the heart of incredulity lies a horror at their apocalyptic nature. The scene has sometimes been seen as a weakness, but in fact this is one of the most disturbing moments of any Middleton play. *The Revenger's Tragedy*, *The Triumphs of Truth*, *A Chaste Maid in Cheapside* and *Women Beware Women* are major achievements, but the latter is supreme amongst the solo works because of its complexity, invention and the daring nature of its dramaturgy.

If the city comedies show a writer attempting to come to terms with rapidly changing social and economic conditions, the tragedies and tragicomedies, with their court settings, reveal a politically involved writer, as critics since Heinemann have shown. Though her concept of 'opposition drama' has been questioned, by revisionist historians in particular, the work of numerous critics since Heinemann has steadily revealed an increasingly detailed picture of Middleton as a political writer, and developed a more complex and subtle understanding of this aspect of his work. Attention has been paid to details of court and city politics: simplistic notions of city/court opposition, for example, have had to be relinquished in the face of a more detailed understanding of business relations between city merchants and courtiers. Recognition of both court and city as sites of competing interests, of negotiation between different power groups, has demanded a more subtle analysis of the orientation of political plays. Examination of censorship has led to scrutiny of textual details from the perspective of the censor-collaborator, revealing politically sensitive material in a play such as *The Lady's Tragedy*, for instance.[22] Indeed, there is hardly a single Middleton play from 1611 onwards that has not been shown to engage with political matters in some respect, usually religious conflict or the scandals connected with Frances Howard, and the same is true of collaborative plays such as *The Old Law* (1618) and *The Changeling* (1622); even an apparently innocuous comedy such as *Anything for a Quiet Life* (1621).[23] *The Witch* and *A Game at Chess* are possibly for us the least dramatically interesting of Middleton texts because their political material is so overt and their topicality emphatic. On the other hand, plays such as *Women Beware Women* or *The Changeling*, though they clearly were contributions to contemporary debates, can successfully engage a twenty-first-century audience who know little or nothing of those matters. But Middleton and his contemporaries were not writing for the future; indeed, they often seem to have been hurrying to finish a play to capitalize on particular events or to catch the mood of the moment, as appears to be the case with *The Witch* and *A Game at Chess*. To do this above all they needed to rely on a collaborative audience to make contemporary meanings.

# 2

# Collaboration

Since the beginnings of modern scholarship in the eighteenth century critics have placed a high value on authorship. This is hardly surprising, for the scholar's primary task is to secure the provenance of texts. The concept has provided both a point of origin and a source of authority, retrieval of an author's intentions regarded as key to establishing the text itself, if not to determine meaning. If one definition of 'the modern' is the rise and privileging of the individual consciousness, it is perhaps not surprising that the consecration of the author occurs at this historical moment. The shift from 'writer' to 'author' draws in its wake an entire legal and philosophical belief system, and it is hardly an exaggeration to suggest it is on this foundation that modern literary scholarship rests.

However, when 'the author' is historicized, the matter becomes complicated. If this figure is a modern construct, not a given or natural entity, then the question that must be asked is how useful it is to apply it to other historical epochs. For much of the twentieth century this issue did not arise, but recently this has been challenged, as a result of two developments, one directly concerned with early modern theatre scholarship, and the other with its origins in postmodern literary theory. Indeed, some aspects of postmodern theory find in the early modern period interesting analogues with the present. One such is the issue of the relationship between writer and text, the other, to be discussed more fully in the next section, the nature of early modern playmaking.

The seminal essay in the shift in literary studies to text-centred interpretation – the recognition that textual meaning changes through time, as a result of the text's activation by successive and different readerships – is Roland Barthes's 'The Death of the Author' (1968). Barthes's essay empowers the reader/critic at the expense of the author, who is to be displaced from the interpretative equation. In emphasizing this shift from a personal, authorial *work* to a *text* open to repeated reinterpretation, Barthes's essay signalled a paradigm shift in literary studies. Michel Foucault's essay 'What is an Author?' (1969) proceeded to ask how an author's name signifies, and concluded that a name imposes a unity and form on texts, restricting textual meaning by its very activation: 'The author is the principle of thrift in the proliferation of meaning'.[1] For Barthes and Foucault the author is an ideological construct, never a neutral device; and, crucially, this construct restricts meaning, as a means of (critical) control and interpretation. Most importantly for us, however, the modern notion of authorship is extremely problematic when applied to early modern playmaking.

**EARLY MODERN THEATRE PRODUCTION**

The comparatively recent move towards a historicist interpretation of drama, with the concomitant emphasis on the materiality of culture, together with a wider shift in theatre studies more generally towards a performance-oriented criticism – a recognition that theatre is above all concerned with the act of performance – has refocused attention on the ways plays are produced and experienced. The excavation of the remains of the Rose playhouse in 1989, and the building of a playhouse based on what is known (and conjectured) of the architecture of the Globe, symbolize two strands of current scholarship: archaeological research into the early modern theatres themselves and the attempt to 'recover', as far as possible, the original conditions of production, and the emphasis on a performance- and reception-based criticism that stresses the historical and political contexts in which these plays operated. Of the many results of this reorientation, one of the most important has been a re-examination of the process by which plays came into being.

If one of the main trends is the shift from a 'literary' to a 'theatrical' approach (to simplify matters for a moment), one key site of tension is the component that straddles and links the two camps: the text itself. The text, in its various forms, is differently constituted as both a written text to be read and an actable text to be performed, and therein lies an important crux. One of the most fertile areas for debate at present is the nature of the text, the role of the writer, and the ways a text changes in the course of its passage from its gestation to its various destinations – stage, printing house, private dwelling. As recent research has shown, questioning some of the assumptions on which much modern scholarship is based reveals a more complex, confusing and ambiguous picture than was previously supposed. Since this debate concerns the very nature and indeed constitution of the text, it is directly relevant to the present discussion to ask, rhetorically: 'What is an author's name? How does it function?'[2]

Scholars working in this field immediately encounter challenges familiar to historians: the problem of evidence. This extends not only to what has survived (thus inviting speculation as to what has not), but to how this evidence may be interpreted. With regard to the working environment of the early modern playhouse we 'know' a good deal, and this will be rehearsed in what follows; but in the gaps that inevitably appear there is scope for speculation and considerable disagreement. From the fortuitous survival of the records kept by Philip Henslowe we have invaluable information about how a playhouse (in this case the Rose, and later the Fortune) operated. Henslowe's *Diary* can tell us much about how the repertory system worked during the years 1594–1604: how popular some plays were, and how frequently they were revived; playhouse income and expenditure; information about plays that have not survived, and the names of dramatists and plays with which they were associated. Whether the *Diary* ought to be taken as representative of accounting and playhouse/company-management generally, or considered solely as a specific case, what it does allow the scholar is an insight, albeit a clouded one, into a significant part of the process that brought plays into being.

A materialist approach to plays recognizes that playmaking was driven primarily by commercial imperatives. Henslowe was an investor, not a wealthy dilettante, and building playhouses was an expensive business. This is important because it puts the nature of playmaking, and the position of the writer, into context. Dramatists were commissioned to compose plays or contribute parts, either to new plays or to old plays for revival. Writers were usually paid in instalments, a portion up front and the remainder upon completion. The manuscript submitted, though so designed, was not properly a *play* at this stage; or, we might say, it was a 'literary' text yet to receive its 'theatrical' realization. For it was up to the actors to render the text actable. No doubt writers who contributed scripts regularly to the same company were familiar with its particular requirements, but a script would in any case be subject to the specific performance capabilities of the company. For a script to be realized would require actors, of course, but not simply a crude number but the appropriate *type* (those who could play women, for example, or juvenile roles, or clowns), and costumes (the most valuable property a company owned), and would be subject to the logistical constraints the venue(s) offered.

Once the writer(s) had submitted the script, it was subject to alteration, if necessary, by two bodies: the Master of the Revels, on the one hand, and the actors, on the other. It is for this reason that the current debate on the relationship between writer and text is so significant. On this matter rests not only textual production and (to use the modern term) authorship, but also the very nature of the text itself, and, looking further afield, the issue of provenance and the canon. All texts required a licence for performance and (where relevant) publication. The Master of the Revels would read a text and indicate on the script any matters he objected to, and these would have to be altered. It was then up to the actors to take the script into rehearsal and render it actable. Only now was it a 'play' in any meaningful sense. What is key here, however, is the position and role of the writer during this process. If the writer's involvement ends with the submission of the script (for which he receives final payment), then the script that leaves his hands is not only no longer his property (it now belongs to the company); it also may be somewhat different from the *play* realized in performance. The Master of the Revels may have demanded changes, and/or the actors may have altered the text to suit their needs. Indeed, the possibility of textual alteration does not end there, for, though it was forbidden to extemporise in performance, it is well known that clowns in particular added material of their own.

With little conclusive evidence for or against, it has been argued that writers continued to play a role in the form the text took, both for the stage and, later, if the play was published; conversely, other scholars have relegated the writer to a marginal, less powerful role than his modern counterpart enjoys, in consequence challenging the very basis of the application of the author figure to early modern drama. These two approaches, one adhering to a modern theory of authorship, the other proposing a collective and decentralized mode of theatrical production, are not absolute models, however: they do not necessarily work for every instance. Clearly playwrights did not enjoy equal status or influence. Shakespeare, most obviously, as both a playwright and a sharer in the Chamberlain's (later King's) Men, almost certainly had more influence than some other writers. It is perhaps unlikely that actors made changes to a script by Shakespeare without either his knowledge or his approval, and actor-writers like Shakespeare and William Rowley may have had input at this stage. Yet even here the picture is uncertain: Ben Jonson complained about changes made in the performance of *Every Man out of his Humour*, for example.[3] If Shakespeare was the exception, rather than the norm, it would seem that the majority of writers did not play a significant role in what happened to the script they sold. If a company decided to publish a play (in so doing effectively relinquishing the monopoly they enjoyed over its performance), it is by no means clear that the writer would reappear to oversee its translation into print. Yet here again the picture is confusing. Jonson clearly played a major role in the publication of his *Workes* in 1616, and makes clear the animus he felt towards actors: the texts he collates are, he informs the reader, stripped of some of the material that appeared in performance. But Jonson is surely an exception who proves the rule: plays were not regarded as 'proper' literature (when Bodley began his library at Oxford plays were excluded); Jonson's publishing initiative exposed him to ridicule. When plays were published, it was a matter decided by the company, and it was the company's name, rather than the dramatist's, that signified on the title page. Even when publishers and companies began to capitalize on a writer's fame (sometimes using a 'name' like Shakespeare's to shift a play written by someone else), the title page signified the collaboration between company, dramatist(s), playhouse (and indeed audience) and printer, rather than, as we might assume, focused on 'authorship' as such. The printing of plays, and their format, can mislead us into moving all too easily from the collaborative world of playmaking to the (modern) world of author recognition.

Two contexts coincide here, the theatrical and the literary. As plays go into print, they move from the theatrical sphere to the literary, from the world of public spectators to that of private readers. It is necessary, then, to consider how the printing of texts did serve to promote authorship. Certainly Jonson's *Workes* and the Shakespeare first folio (1623) did precisely this (the latter posthumously). Whereas writers were not directly associated with plays as performed, at least not textually, for playbills advertised play, company and venue, printers sometimes exploited a name to shift copies. If writers were very much behind the scenes, theatrically speaking, they were 'named' in print. In terms of printed texts, then, it can be argued that, in Foucauldian terms, writers are beginning to be ideologically constructed in the early decades of the seventeenth century.[4] Yet it is to be doubted whether we should speak of an *author* in the playhouse, not only for the likelihood that the majority of writers exerted very little control over what happened to texts once they had sold them to a company, but equally importantly because these texts live on beyond the natural life of their creator(s), and were subject to subsequent change and alteration.

This text/authorship issue produces a seeming impasse that pivots on the theatre/literature opposition. However, a more useful category might yet emerge. It may be that collaboration offers both a means of deconstructing the text/author opposition, and a historically-pertinent trope through which to understand early modern theatrical production.

## TEXT AND PROVENANCE

Scholars have privileged single authorship in part, as we have seen, because the concept has been central to theories of editing, and in part because Shakespeare has been considered *sui generis* for his exemplary genius as sole author of plays. Yet the assumption that Shakespeare did not collaborate is demonstrably false, and the denigration of dramatists who did paints a most misleading picture of early modern playmaking. Jeffrey Masten argues that single authorship is a misleading category, since it sets up a collaboration/sole composition opposition. He deconstructs this model, proposing that the notion of *sole* authorship is undermined by the evidence, which suggests a *culture* of collaboration that overdetermines *all* forms of textual production.[5] It may be necessary then to rethink collaboration both as central to the operation of the playhouse and as a model that defines the culture of early modern literary production both specifically and generally. That is, collaboration can also serve to deconstruct the literature/theatre opposition identified earlier. G. E. Bentley's conclusion that up to half of the plays written during the period 1590–1642 were the work of more than one writer might be taken, statistically, to argue a joint case, for both collaboration and sole authorship as distinctive modes of composition.[6] But, as Masten argues, 'authorship' carries with it assumptions inapplicable to the early modern period. Citing a range of recent studies, he points out that, whereas moderns privilege originality, early moderns practised imitation – in writing style and handwriting, for example – and the modern notion of intellectual property would make no sense to writers for whom use of textual matter, implicitly held in common, could in the modern sense only be considered plagiarism.[7] Since authorship is *individual* in make-up, the collective, communal nature of theatrical production poses considerable problems for the paradigm. Crucially, even 'sole' composition is characterized by writing practices that are in essence collaborative.

Composition was not a straightforward matter: the text was a communal product, an open text susceptible to alteration. But more than this, as a text it was composed of layers of meaning that activated, and were activated by, another interpretative community, the playhouse audience. No writer composes in a vacuum, and dramatists drew on past and contemporary influences and narratives; the resulting text comprised numerous voices, a palimpsest of influences, echoes and intertextual allusions. This composite text, complex in origin, 'written up' by dramatist(s) and actors, censored by the Master of the Revels, was in turn interpreted by actors, whose very playing was both a reading of the script and a rewriting of it in a different medium. The resulting performance was a collaborative ensemble production, made possible by a company of actors who collectively interpreted the text. All theatre is collaborative; in the early modern playhouse this extended to a production of meaning with multiple rather than single origins. Indeed, if textual origins are ultimately elusive, since so many voices had an input, it is perhaps more useful to think of these texts as having *no* discernible origin as such, but a multiplicity of contributors.

If Bentley's contention that '*every* performance in the commercial theatres from 1590 to 1642 was essentially an act of collaboration' is accepted,[8] then even assumptions about exceptions need to be re-examined. As Stephen Orgel remarks, Shakespeare 'was simply in on more parts of the collaboration'.[9] In his important essay 'What is a Text?', written in 1981, Orgel suggests that the reason Jonson alters his texts for publication is 'precisely because he hasn't sufficient *authority* in the theatrical versions'.[10] Echoing Bentley's reminder that playwrights did not necessarily provide the subjects of the plays they were commissioned to write or contribute to (in many cases the company may have stipulated what kind of play they were looking for, and hired specific dramatists accordingly),[11] Orgel signals the importance of considering how patronage complicates notions of authorship and authority. And, while Jonson may have been able to reassert some control over the text, for most writers this was not the case: 'The publisher was fully entitled to alter the manuscript if he saw fit – the manuscript was his'.[12] A well-known instance of this is the publication in 1590 of the *Tamburlaine* plays, the scripts of which were first written by Christopher Marlowe in the late 1580s. Phenomenally successful, they enjoyed revivals in 1594–5 and later. But the plays as first performed were different from the texts published. The printer Richard Jones declares in his address to the reader:

> I have purposely omitted and left out some fond and frivolous jestures, digressing and, in my poor opinion, far unmeet for the matter, which I thought might seem more tedious unto the wise than any way else to be regarded – though, haply, they have been of some vain conceited fondlings greatly gaped at, what times they were showed upon the stage in their graced deformities.[13]

Jonson's excision of theatrical moments and Marlowe's exclusion from the editing process at the printing stage are examples both of the problems of making assumptions about authorship, and of the ways texts are always, in various ways, collaborative.

This has important implications for the editing of texts, the construction of authorship and the neglect of writers who are, in the light of the foregoing discussion, *incorrectly* termed 'collaborators': all early modern writers, particularly dramatists, were collaborators, in different ways, subject to the forces of patronage, commissioning, adaptation, revision and – now as well as then – editing, which produced a composite text that scholarship oversimplifies by assigning an 'author'. Indeed, if the discussion is taken a stage further, and the process of modern editing and canon formation considered, then we find that the textual issues with which scholars contend are not confined to the early modern period. The revision of texts, both during and immediately after a writer's lifetime, continues to this day, since no text can be considered fixed: readings of words, as much of the provenance of texts, are contested. The quest for the author – through recovery of his 'intentions' – remains a constant, even though early modern dramatic texts are shot through with multiple voices. Only gradually, and belatedly, is recognition of the complexity of composition – and with it the tentative undoing of the notion of *author*ity – being acknowledged. The two *King Lear*s in the Oxford (1986) and Norton Shakespeares (1997), and Arden 3's decision to publish not one but *three Hamlet*s – the quarto and folio texts – are testament to this shift towards a textual pluralism.

If collaboration is the new 'paradigm' that takes into account the material conditions of playmaking at all its various stages, it is important to distinguish further between different *forms* of collaboration. We have broadened out the concept of 'collaboration' to include the various stages a text went through during its passage from manuscript to playhouse and, in many cases, printing house. But within the categories 'collaborative writer' and 'collaborative writing' there is a range of activities.

Unfortunately, if unsurprisingly, very little information about precise writing practices has survived, so scholars can only hypothesize about how plays were written. What is fairly clear is that collaborative writing, understood as the joint composition of a manuscript between two or more contributors, must have ranged from a division of labour into equal shares, from the beginning when the play was commissioned to its delivery to the actors, to a practice where one dramatist might take a more senior role in overseeing the collaboration. Certainly playwrights at the beginning of their careers contributed scenes or parts of dialogue that more experienced writers then fitted into the play. A common scenario involved the commissioning of a single writer, who might then 'subcontract' the commission to one or more other writers, perhaps because he was pressed for time, or because he wanted a writer expert at clown scenes, for example, to contribute a particular scene or subplot. Whether, in any of these cases, the 'final' assembly of the text was a truly collaborative effort between all involved, or whether a single writer took responsibility, is not known; in all likelihood variations on all these scenarios happened at one time or another.

This question of writing practices leads to a further issue, for it might seem that collaborative writing can itself be broken down into components of *solo* composition. Where collaborative playwriting has received attention, there has often been an urge to 'disintegrate' texts, to divide texts according to their component parts/'authors'. As should be apparent, the present study is not concerned with this aim, for it quite clearly signals a return to the authorship paradigm with which we take issue. In the chapters that follow we are interested primarily in the ways collaborative texts function, not with a quest to 'find the author', though such scholarship is essential when attempting to identify the canon of a playwright. Indeed, statistical and computer analysis of linguistic traits has been essential for work on Thomas Middleton.[14] Determining Middleton's hand in texts is by definition 'disintegrationist', for it relies chiefly on the premiss that writers have linguistic signatures (grammar, spelling, word use) through which their presence in a text may be detected. However, while computer-aided analysis may well increase the possibility of identifying a given writer's involvement in composing a specific text, it is important to recognize that for many collaborators the process was likely to have been genuinely collaborative, rather than a variation on the theme of single authorship. Writers may, or may not, have written 'side by side', but, just as dramatists familiar with a particular company would tailor their work to suit, they would also, presumably, 'accommodate' the writing of their collaborators. 'Accommodation theory' proposes that plays need not necessarily be regarded as an amalgam of *different* voices.[15] Perhaps this might be the case with a first draft, but the process of collaborative composition, the marrying-together of components, characters and stage business, would suggest plausibly that writers reworked not only their 'own' text to fit in with others', but also revised that of others. It seems highly unlikely that dramatists did not comment on others' contributions, make suggestions, or partly rewrite, and they may have done so in forms and ways that *accommodated* their colleagues' verbal tics or linguistic preferences. They may, indeed, have adopted a different, *non-authorial* style. The more one looks at collaboration, the more it is necessary to regard it as a fluid process – a diachronic activity whose end result, the 'finished' text, is arrived at following multiple interventions and compromises. For us, accommodation theory is an important corrective to the disintegrationist approach.

If revisions took place during the writing of a play, before (and indeed after) it reached the players, revision also happened later, and sometimes long afterwards. Here is where the term 'author' is doubly inadequate when applied to collaboration, for it suggests that *only* authors themselves were involved in the composition of 'their' plays. Henslowe's *Diary* makes it clear that plays were sometimes later revised for revival. Dramatists were commissioned to add material, to extend a play's life and to appeal to new audiences. Here is further evidence that a text's life was not connected by umbilical cord to its creator(s): revision took several forms, including a writer's revision of a script he had initially helped compose; but writers also revised texts that were new to them. Sometimes writers who had been responsible for the original scripts were dead, as is the case with Marlowe and *Doctor Faustus*, of which the two extant texts (1604, 1616) were printed years after his death. While scholars and publishers agree *Doctor Fautus* is 'Marlowe's' play, this is a convenient fiction that masks the complexities of textual production and erases the realities of collaboration and revision.

Revisions could also be adaptations. But the term brings us to a specific category of collaboration, which the dramatist's departure, not simply in the abstract terms of 'author' but, as with Marlowe, as a consequence of his death, introduces, and which once again highlights the importance of the text: posthumous collaboration. Strictly speaking of course this is a sleight of hand. But it is important to recognize that, like all dramatists, Middleton turned to texts left behind by dead writers. Stephen Greenblatt famously remarked that his interest in early modern literature 'began with a desire to speak with the dead'.[16] It is, for all scholars of the past, a reasonable rationale. However we read, and reuse, texts, we do so to bring them 'to life'. The revision of 'dead' texts has a similarly Lazarus-like aim, even if the result is sometimes a Frankenstein's monster. But the analogy is not inappropriate, for, if all texts are patchworks of past and contemporary utterances, breathing life into fragments and sewing them together, the posthumous collaboration should surely be regarded as a further collaborative act, at the level of the text. After all, only texts can speak, as the first editors of the Shakespeare folio recognized when they declared their aim to be 'onely to keepe the memory of so worthy a Friend, & Fellow alive'.[17] And, of course, this the King's Men did, above all, in the collaborative act of theatre.

## COLLABORATIVE MIDDLETON

T. S. Eliot was troubled by what he called Middleton's lack of 'personality': 'He has no point of view, is neither sentimental nor cynical; he is neither resigned, nor disillusioned, nor romantic, he has no message. He is merely the name which associates six or seven great plays.'[18] Eliot's concern is with the 'disappearance' of the author into the collaborative texts from which his voice cannot be disentangled. After Barthes and Foucault, few would sympathize with Eliot's view; indeed, critics argue strongly that Middleton did indeed have a 'message', if by this we are to understand that his plays frequently participate in social and political debates. But the kind of textual openness and ambiguity Eliot touches on here has also been echoed, the plays' very resistance to resolving the questions they raise leading to comparisons with the drama of the twentieth-century dramatist Bertolt Brecht.[19] It is perhaps, then, more useful to turn Eliot's criticism on its head, for, as we saw in the previous chapter, Middleton's career demonstrates his flexibility and skill in turning his hand to myriad themes and genres.

The first we hear of Middleton as a playwright is in Henslowe's *Diary*. An entry dated 22 May 1602 records payment to 'Anthony Munday & Michael Drayton, Webster & the rest Middleton in earnest of a Book called *Caesar's Fall*',[20] and a week later these four, with Thomas Dekker, receive the final installment. Less than six months later Middleton appears again, this time alone; he receives an advance on 21 October and the final payment, totalling £6, on 9 November for *Randall Earl of Chester*. Unfortunately neither text survives. Just over a month later he contributes a new prologue and epilogue for a court performance of *Friar Bacon and Friar Bungay*, written by Robert Greene, who had been dead for a decade. From this evidence, in a little over six months Middleton had established himself, contributing to both the Admiral's Men and Worcester's Men, working alone and with other playwrights/texts. It was a pattern that was to be repeated throughout his career, a career that was remarkable rather than unusual.

With the exception of Marlowe and Chapman, Middleton collaborated with all the prominent dramatists of the age, including Jonson, who thought him 'but a base fellow'.[21] While scholars continue to debate the precise extent of his collaborative relationships, the names of Dekker, Drayton, Fletcher, Ford, Heywood, Massinger, Munday, Rowley, Shakespeare and Webster have all been associated with Middleton. If this supports Eliot's remark that he 'collaborated shamelessly',[22] it more accurately testifies not only to the realities of early modern theatre but to his skill as a playwright and, indeed, his prominence among his contemporaries. If, unlike Thomas Heywood, he did not (so far as we know) claim to have had a hand in 220 plays,[23] he is a crucial figure in early modern drama because of the sheer quality of the plays he wrote jointly with others. In terms of his range and influence, and perhaps most significantly his 'collaborative revisioning' of myriad features of early modern culture, Middleton is certainly one of the most important writers in the Jacobean theatre.

Middleton's range, flexibility and skill are writ small in the chronology assembled at the beginning of this study. For reasons of space we focus on the major professional relationships Middleton enjoyed, and the following three chapters correspondingly explore the plays he wrote with Dekker, Shakespeare and Rowley respectively. The chronology simplifies a complex grid of association connecting the key components of the early modern theatre: writer(s), acting company, playhouse. The chronological account reveals Middleton's breadth and reminds us of the difficulty facing the scholar who seeks to impose a 'pattern' on this playwright's career in particular. Yet, if the intersections between Middleton and these three playwrights are traced, a pattern – or patterns – may be discerned. As we shall see, these relationships, extending throughout Middleton's professional life, direct us in turn to what is, with hindsight, a perfectly logical and striking feature of Middleton drama: the frequent intertextual connections between texts, both within the collaborations and across the Middleton canon itself. As the following discussions illustrate, Middleton and collaboration are inseparable, even when Middleton's 'own' plays are considered in isolation. In Dekker, Shakespeare and Rowley Middleton cultivated important artistic relationships, but they all had in common a trait central to Middleton drama: an intertextual, reflexive, essentially palimpsestic approach to the writing, production and reception of early modern drama.

# 3

# Middleton and Dekker

Thomas Dekker (1572–1626) was an established playwright when Middleton arrived in London. Indeed, his 1599 play *Old Fortunatus* may have inspired the name of the newly opened Fortune playhouse in 1600.[1] Between 1598 and 1602 he 'wrote all or parts of 44 different plays for Henslowe'[2] – a remarkable, though perhaps not exceptional, rate of production. One, now lost, was *Caesar's Fall* (1602), the first in which Middleton had a hand. Plague closed the playhouses in 1603: in response, Middleton and Dekker produced two pamphlets, *News from Gravesend* and *The Meeting of Gallants at an Ordinary*, followed by their first surviving collaboration; in spring 1604 Henslowe records a payment 'unto Thomas Dekker & Middleton in earnest of their play called *The Patient Man and the Honest Whore*'.[3] The year 1604 was productive and prestigious for both men: with Stephen Harrison and Ben Jonson they contributed to *The Whole Royal and Magnificent Entertainment Given to King James through the City of London* to celebrate the new monarch's entry into the capital. Both wrote pageants independently: *Troia Nova Triumphans* (Dekker, 1612) and *The Triumphs of Truth* (Middleton, 1613) are considered the highest achievements of the genre. In addition to *The Bloody Banquet* (1608–9), their names are linked with those of John Ford, William Rowley and a 1623 play, *The Spanish Gypsy*, but it is for *The Roaring Girl* (1611), which draws on Dekker's pamphlets on canting and dramatizes the life of a famous contemporary figure, that they are remembered together.

In the case of a sustained collaborative relationship it is tempting to speculate on the precise nature of the partnership. One reason these two dramatists repeatedly worked together was their compatibility, though whether by this we might infer they were similar in outlook, or rather that their differences combined to produce an aesthetic greater than the sum of its parts, is a matter of conjecture. Certainly, like many of their countrymen, they had one belief in common: fear of Spain and suspicion of Rome, a concern that increased markedly during the reign of James I. Dekker's *The Whore of Babylon* (1605) has been described as 'the definitive militant Protestant play',[4] and in pamphlets and plays Dekker's support for the poor is apparent, suggesting that 'his work echoes the factional and class politics of a radical Protestant opposition'.[5] Like Middleton, he was drawn to overtly religious material, publishing a prayer collection, *The Four Birds of Noah's Ark*, in 1609. Undoubtedly, a shared political consciousness was one ingredient in the complex mix out of which their plays emerged.

If compatibility was important for the partnership's long-term prospects, more significant, certainly in the beginning, were the institutional playwriting practices that brought them together. Like Middleton, Dekker wrote for the Admiral's/Prince Henry's and Worcester's Men in the 1590s and early 1600s, and both were to write for the most successful company of the era, the Chamberlain's/King's Men. Their careers followed similar paths. They were in a position at the turn of the century to capitalize on the demand for plays by the children's companies, writing for Paul's Boys, and both produced pamphlets when plague closed the theatres in 1603,[6] Dekker *The Wonderful Yeare* (1603) and Middleton *The Black Book* (1604). More than any of their contemporaries, they took London as their subject, reflecting but more importantly *refracting* London, showing it in its many guises, good and ill.

## MIDDLETON, DEKKER, LONDON

The London of Middleton and Dekker is a city of sharp practices, of victims and villains, tricksters and gulls, staples of the new city comedy that satirized both the nouveau poor aristocracy and the emerging mercantile class, whose arriviste social aspirations were widely lampooned. In plays such as Dekker's *The Shoemaker's Holiday* (1599) and Middleton's *A Trick to Catch the Old One* (1605) the social realities of London's dog-eat-dog economy form the backdrop of romantic plot lines that resolve, or apparently resolve, class and gender conflicts that modern critics, and early modern spectators perhaps, in turn reposition offstage. Thus dramas that often offer reconciliation do so only after drawing attention to the causes of conflict, and in evoking a recognizable offstage world invite playgoers to view their own, small world writ large.

As the title in Henslowe's *Diary* indicates, *1 Honest Whore* (1604) juxtaposes plots featuring a citizen with inexhaustible patience and a whore who turns honest. Evidently the play was popular, for Dekker wrote a sequel, both plays exploring themes they were to exploit throughout their careers: power, madness, corruption, class division and gender relations. Indeed, several overlapping correspondences can be detected in Middleton's *The Phoenix* (1604): it is similarly set in Italy (Ferrara); Quieto is like the patient man, and in a familiarly Middletonian jibe at the law Tangle is so litigious that he goes mad. The setting in the collaborative play is Milan, which like other Italian cities playgoers associated with vice and corruption. Here the Duke's determination that his daughter Infelice will not marry her lover Hippolyto leads him to give out that she has died; drugged, she is then spirited away and told her suitor has perished. From the outset, anticipating the scenario of *The Revenger's Tragedy*, the court is depicted as tyrannous, oppressive; where the later play results in murder and mayhem, however, comedy is the dominant mode here. Although the play begins and ends with the Duke surrounded by his court, the Milan locale competes with the two principals of the title. Despite their Italian names, Candido, the 'patient man', and Bellafront, the 'honest whore', establish the play's London coordinates, and a familiar portrait of merchants and gallants ensues. Viola's frustration with her husband's docility reaches a climax when gallants wager they can make him angry, only to find themselves invited to dinner; eventually she has Candido certified, setting up the final madhouse scene which looks forward to *The Changeling*. Indeed, *1 Honest Whore* is throughout concerned with alteration and corruption. Hippolyto's condemnation of Bellafront –

>           your body,
> Its like the common shoare that still receiues
> All the townes filth.
>
> (*HW* II. i. 324-6)

– evokes the familiar anti-theatre charge, linking the cheek-by-jowl playhouses and brothels in the liberties,[7] as in Henry Crosse's diatribe in *Vertues Commonwealth* (1603) that 'a Play is like a sincke in a Towne, whereunto all the filth doth runne: or a byle in the body, that draweth all the ill humours unto it'.[8] Chastened, Bellafront falls in love with Hippolyto, and turns away from vice:

>                          by my example,
> I hope few maydens now will put their heads
> Vnder mens girdeles.
>
> (*HW* III. iii. 124-6)

This raises a question at the centre of the play: is the moralistic tone here endorsed, or is the prevailing mode satirical? Locating the play in the *commedia dell'arte* tradition points to *1 Honest Whore* satirizing Candido and his class;[9] alternatively, he may be read as a positive affirmation of that class, his triumphing over the gallants a celebration of merchant power.[10] That both readings are possible – the play as 'simultaneously an exclamation and a critique of civic power and the ethos of the City'[11] – is testament to the richness of textual and contextual associations available to playgoers, as well as diversity among critics.

Bellafront has been at the service of members of the court, not least Matheo, 'the first [who] | Gaue money for my soule' (*HW* III. iii. 94-5). If the Duke's deceit and plot to murder Hippolyto provide a dark undercurrent, Candido's scenes maintain the play's levity, measure for measure. The gallants' attempts to rile him would have been met with laughter and applause, the audience privileged to enjoy the discomforting of both social groups. Thus the exchange between a gallant and a whore –

> CASTRUCHIO. What an asse is that lord, to borrow money of a Citizen.
> BELLAFRONT. Nay, Gods my pitty, what an asse is that Citizen to lend mony to a lord.
>
> (*HW* II. i. 115-17)

– is a nice joke for spectators but it signals an economic reality not far beneath the surface of the play.

This playful tone sews together the threads of a plot whose undertone frequently glances at 'reality', offstage. That Candido must be mad to resist so much provocation results in his being sent to the madhouse, proven by an equally logical Catch 22:

CANDIDO. What? am I mad say you, and I not know it?
OFFICER. That proues you mad, because you know it not.
(*HW* IV. iii. 158–9)

But, as with *The Changeling*, the madhouse scenes play on the role of disguise and tap into the vogue for treating madmen as theatre, here evoking 'Bedlam' or Bethlehem hospital.[12] The disguising at the close, the Duke and his lieutenants closing in on the escaped lovers as they plan a clandestine marriage, anticipates the murderous masquing of *The Revenger's Tragedy*, but madness is preferred to massacre: 'none goes to be married till he be starke mad' (*HW* V. ii. 35). Confirmation of this shift is signalled when the Duke's party voluntarily surrenders its weapons to the friar, and the only violence is a mock-killing involving two madmen. Fittingly, Bellafront is the agent of resolution, unmasking herself and the lovers; forced to accept that his daughter is now married, the Duke in turn commands Matheo to marry Bellafront, a decree that parallels the Duke's order to Angelo and Lucio in another 1604 play, *Measure for Measure*.

Candido is a linen-draper, and in one scene, deprived of his senatorial cloak, he dons a rug, seemingly impervious to the social significance of dress and, of course, resistant to his wife's attempts to rile him. Even when his servant appears dressed as the master, his response is to complete the exchange and dress in servants' clothes. Here the play rehearses a commonplace about the role of costume and role-playing in the theatre, but its social significance would not have been lost on playgoers, for whom the wearing of colours and fabrics was regulated according to station, even though the sumptuary legislation brought in during Elizabeth's reign was repealed in 1604.[13] The fluidity of attire on stage both re-enacted the rapid social and economic change in early modern England that city comedy dramatized, and served to remind spectators of the semiotics of dress. For some commentators the breaching of regulations posed a threat to social order: Phillip Stubbes in *The Anatomie of Abuses* (1583) fulminated against the 'confuse[d] mingle mangle of apparell'[14] caused not only by social aspirants but by women who dressed in male attire.[15] In *1 Honest Whore* little is at stake, but when Middleton and Dekker returned to the topic, and to the Fortune, some years later, the issue was centre stage.

## THE ROARING GIRL

Textual analysis suggests *1 Honest Whore* was a 'very close collaboration';[16] to an even greater extent *The Roaring Girl* was a joint composition. Although attempts have been made to identify a scene/hand correspondence,[17] 'most scenes reveal evidence of both dramatists'.[18] Whether they actually composed side by side, or revised each other's work, cannot be ascertained, but 'the progress from composition to the stage and finally into print was a comparatively swift one',[19] indicating an integrative process during which 'a less formal, freer division of responsibilities may well have evolved'.[20] We ought perhaps not to be surprised that the high point of their partnership should result from such close cooperation.

The play's subject is, in diverse ways, a collaborative presence. The inspiration for the protagonist was a young woman called Mary Frith, notorious for her unconventional behaviour. Early in 1612, only months after the play was staged,[21] *The Consistory of London Correction Book* records that Frith 'voluntarily confessed *tha*t she had long frequented all or most of the disorderly & licentious pla*ces* in this Cittie as namely she hath vsually in the habite of a man resorted to alehowses Tavernes Tobacco shops & also to play howses there to see plaies'.[22]

The regulating of women in early modern England is well documented. As for men, one form of ordering women was restricting what they could wear; going in disguise as a man was in some circumstances safer, particularly when travelling alone (a theme exploited in plays). However, it was also associated with lewd behaviour. Frith admits to going to 'all or most of the disorderly and licentious pla*ces* in this Cittie' – code for prostitution. It is significant that lumped into this list of disreputable venues and activities are playhouses and playgoing: to its detractors, such as the Church and City authorities, the theatre encouraged immoral behaviour, and the association of playing, playgoing and prostitution was commonplace, as Hippolyto's charge against Bellafront illustrates. Frith's 'crime' (cross-dressing was not illegal[23]) was to masquerade 'in the fashion of a man with a mans cloake on her to the great scandall of diuers persons who vnderstood the same & to the disgrace of all womanhood'[24] – a perfectly picaresque figure for playwrights expert in writing about the city. Critics have been similarly intrigued by a play that explores the politics of dress and desire in early modern England – both on- and offstage. A key question is how precisely the wider significance of the regulation of dress interplays with all-male acting conventions[25] – an issue that is inseparable from the practicalities of early modern theatre practice, but that is occasionally placed centre stage, as in Middleton's *The Widow* (1615), where Martia is involved in multiple cross-dressings and gender confusions. *The Roaring Girl*, however, is a rather exceptional case. As we shall see, Middleton and Dekker's play explores the intersection of theatre and city by focusing on how clothing signifies class and gender identity, and yet simultaneously registers a system of social ordering under pressure from socio-economic change. Crucially, though, it does so in a metatheatrical 'representing' of a figure whose offstage performances are themselves theatrical events.

Befitting its subject, the play is a witty economy of visual and verbal exchange, like *1 Honest Whore* combining the staples of city comedy with a conventional romance plot. Ostensibly, Moll Cutpurse's role is to facilitate a marriage to thwart a mean parent, against a backdrop of the familiar jostling for position (a *double entendre* entirely in keeping with the text's wordplay) between citizen and gallant. In the face of Sir Alexander's Wengrave's opposition, his son Sebastian seeks to marry Mary Fitz-Allard, a pattern of conflict between generations Middleton explores elsewhere, such as *A Trick to Catch the Old One* and *A Chaste Maid in Cheapside* (1613). In keeping with Frith's reputation, Moll brings to the world of the citizen and gallant the 'underworld' of the cutpurse, the play drawing directly on Dekker's 1608 pamphlets *The Belman of London* and *Lantern and Candle-Light*.[26] On one plane the play's driving force is sexual desire, whether in terms of marriage (Sebastian and Mary) or simply lust (the gallants' pursuit of the citizens' wives, and Laxton's of Moll); indeed, Sebastian and Laxton are titillated by Mary and Moll respectively in male attire.[27] But the play is as much concerned with class as it is with the issues of gender and desire that Moll's presence raises.[28] Mary's dowry is insufficient to satisfy Sir Alexander's appetite for money and status; the gallants' behaviour tropes the aristocratic hunt, their quarry fair game, playthings bored by marriage to dull 'apron husbands' (*RG* III. ii. 33), all three of whom in part recall Candido in *1 Honest Whore*. But Moll is outside the structuring templates of these two categories: if to some characters she is of uncertain gender, her class position is similarly amorphous. In the carefully policed boundaries of both she is at least potentially a threat. She toys with Laxton, whose name 'lack-stone', where stone is slang for testicle,[29] signals that he is not fully a man. Moll and Laxton both make a show of masculine qualities, but when she bests him in a duel (reworking Viola's encounter with Sir Andrew Aguecheek in *Twelfth Night* (1601)), her demonstration of swordsmanship is a symbolic appropriation of the phallus, as is her playing of a viol in Act IV, Scene i.[30] Equally, while her indeterminate social standing facilitates ease of movement through the strata of the play-world, her role in exposing deceit and intrigue (Laxton, Sir Alexander, as well as the cutpurses) leaves her outside the play's social economy. Ironically, if Moll is finally accepted by the principals at the close, it is in terms of her gender, rather than her class.

Sebastian's plan to use Moll as a decoy, feigning a 'counterfeit passion' (*RG* I. i. 102) for her in the hope that his father will come to view a match with Mary with relief, enlists the support of the knowing audience. Sir Alexander's response registers both horror and the kind of anxiety Stubbes expresses in his aptly titled *Anatomie of Abuses*:

> It is a thing
> One knows not how to name: her birth began
> Ere she was all made. 'Tis woman more than man,
> Man more than woman, and – which to none can hap –
> The sun gives her two shadows to one shape.
>
> (*RG* I. ii. 128–32)

Moll has not yet appeared: she is known by report, talked of before her entrance, the play exploiting playgoers' expectations. But the dramatists seek to wrong-foot those in the playhouse, like those on stage, who have preconceptions about Moll. In the Prologue the dramatists acknowledge that each playgoer 'brings a play in's head with him' (l. 4). However, unlike 'suburb-roarers' (l. 21) and 'civil, city-roaring girl[s]' (l. 22) – and unlike Frith – the Moll of the play

> flies
> With wings more lofty. Thus her character lies –
> Yet what need characters, when to give a guess
> Is better than the person to express?
> But would you know who 'tis? Would you hear her name? –
> She is called Mad Moll; her life our acts proclaim!
> 
> (*RG*, Prologue, ll. 25–30)

This 'life our acts proclaim' is not a simulacrum of Frith's reputation as a drunken woman with doubtful morals – the very *image* her cross-dressing affirms. Instead, the play offers a figure both recognizable to the audience and at variance with Frith's notoriety. Like Middleton's later city comedies, *A Chaste Maid in Cheapside*, for example, this play has less of the raw underbelly of London seen in *A Trick to Catch the Old One* or *The Puritan* (1606). Moll is a somewhat romanticized figure in Middleton and Dekker's version, witty and assured rather than marginalized and oppressed. Yet, if Moll's dramatic empowerment makes for a vibrant, energetic play some critics claim pulls its punches, the play resists any critical simplification of the issues and the playwrights' treatment of them.

The main theme is set out in Middleton's address to the reader. 'The fashion of play-making I can properly compare to nothing so naturally as the alteration in apparel' (ll. 1–2), he writes, and proceeds to describe the changing fashions of theatre in terms of attire, determined, in the face of the 'worse things, I must needs confess, the world has taxed her for' (ll. 19–20), that the writer should 'leave things better than he finds 'em' (l. 22). This is interesting not only for the sentiment (meant ironically of course), but because it may offer an insight into the audience's reception of the play. This is not to suggest that the play was a failure in commercial terms, or that it was received negatively. But underneath Middleton's 'quaint conceits' (l. 8) there is at least a suggestion of defensiveness, a reminder to readers that their notion of Mary Frith will not receive automatic confirmation in what they are about to read. The address ends acknowledging that the writers prefer 'a slackness of truth, than fulness of slander' (ll. 29–30).

*The Roaring Girl* exploits the theme of dress at the level of theatre as well as theme: form and content are bound together in the very clothing that articulates meaning – both on- and offstage. Early modern England was 'a cloth society',[31] dependent on a sign system that was also a commercial market[32] – illustrated in the play's depiction of shops and measuring and buying of cloth. In the playhouse this was doubly so, since costumes (often cast-off aristocratic attire) both determined character status and functioned as fluid props interchanged among multi-role actors, who were of course of low rank.[33] On a bare stage, costume was king; but kings were malleable constructs, *made* of cloth: clothes, onstage and off, were a floating signifier, signalling changeability, not stability. If 'the theater seems to stage cloth as the site of a crisis, in which meaning is simultaneously profoundly asserted and denied',[34] *The Roaring Girl* styles such a crisis in terms of both gender and social rank. On one level concerned (most obviously) with cross-dressing, while on the other shot through with socio-economic tensions, the play harnesses and releases desire as a de(con)-structive force that threatens to produce a carnivalesque inversion of social order.

Whether it remains a mere *threat* has been much debated; where there is consensus is in the centrality of dress to the construction of social meaning in the play. For the reader – hardly unsuspecting – the 1611 title-page and woodcut of 'Moll Cutpurse' conjure the textual cross-dressed protagonist in the quoted proverb, 'My cafe is alter'd': 'cafe' (case), meaning clothing – but also vagina – 'alter'd' leading into the sexually allusive 'I muft worke for my liuing'.[35] For the spectator, the theme is established from the outset, when Mary Fitz-Allard enters *'disguised like a sempster, with a case for bands'* (*RG* I.i.0). This is the first of a series of onstage references to dressing, 'bands' here are collars (for Sebastian), but with a pun on the 'marriage banns' linking the two lovers. This is not the play's (or Mary's) only example of disguise, but it is highly significant that Moll never conceals her identity.[36] In her first appearance, '*in a frieze jerkin and a black safeguard*' (*RG* II. i. 174, s.d), she is dressed in male and female attire – a jacket and a riding skirt.[37] In the next scene she is measured for a pair of breeches; when in Act III, Scene i she appears '*like a man*' (*RG* III. i. 37, s.d.) the audience has been prepared, and the tables are turned: it is as 'a man' that Moll humiliates Laxton, and embarks on her plan to 'defy all men, their worst hates|And their best flatteries' (*RG* III. i. 92–3), 'scorn[ing] to prostitute myself to a man,|I that can prostitute a man to me!' (*RG* III. i. 111–12).

Whether Moll's independence and determination to resist the patriarchal imperative to marry – 'He was in fear his son would marry me, |But never dreamt that I would ne'er agree!' (*RG* V. ii. 213–14) – can be read as a victory is a question that tends to divide critics: she does, after all, serve as a *device* to secure the marriage of others. But perhaps this doubleness is the key. In her eye-catching movement through the socially demarcated space of the stage Moll anticipates the *flaneur* of Walter Benjamin's modern city,[38] a figure whose liminal status is alternately a sign of the self-fashioning subject who observes, and the imprisoned object already incorporated into the process of commodification. 'Constantly on view as well as viewing', the *flaneur* 'signal[s] a need to create a different sort of time and space around themselves from the kind of rushing time and crowded space they feel pressing in on them from outside'.[39] Dekker's *The Gull's Hornbook* (1609) has been described as 'a kind of *flaneur*'s handbook',[40] but, while the advice-book satirizes gallants' behaviour, *The Roaring Girl* explores, three-dimensionally, the relationship between language, costume and movement. The play's ambiguous mediation of inside/outside in Moll's social status, the infusion of cutpurse patois into language and the spatial relationships on stage comprise an early modern exploration of the *flaneur*'s self-fashioned alienation from/in the city.

Thus Moll's distance from gallants and citizens in Act II, as she weaves her way through the avenue of shop-booths on stage, dismissive of the frivolities of gallant/citizen (wife) interaction, both mocks the fripperies of feathers and tobacco and situates her in the visible marketplace of fashioning. While for the dramatists Moll is their redefined *subject*, moving through the play's world with witty aplomb, for the audience of the Fortune Moll is the *object* of their gaze – the play's *actual* commodity, subject to conspicuous consumption. Throughout the play these tensions are apparent – Moll's *otherness* (itself paradoxically undercut by her openness as a (wo)man/(char)-actor) always uncannily familiar as well as estranged, antagonist of, yet participant in, city comedy. In a sense this is the play's point – to return to the critical problem of linking (in a play so obviously concerned with such links) the staging of *The Roaring Girl* with the offstage world – for the *flaneur*'s status invites ongoing negotiation, rather than closure. This was certainly the case, for Moll Frith appeared shortly after the play to do penance at St Paul's, as well as (textually) elsewhere, and is biographically conjured half a century later, just after her death. Indeed, for the Fortune's audience, this *flaneur*, this inside/outside, multiply-constructed identity, is brought forth in the moment of performance as a literal manifestation of the figure who, not unlike the gallant sitting onstage, is seen, as well as seeing.

## COLLABORATION AND PERFORMANCE

Sir Alexander's address to the Fortune's audience, likening to the portraits in 'my galleries' (*RG* I. ii. 14) 'a thousand heads' (*RG* I. ii. 19) watching the play, is an oft-quoted moment of metatheatre. In keeping with both anti-theatrical sentiment and his role as Moll's chief antagonist, he imagines seeing 'a cutpurse [who] thrusts and leers|With hawk's eyes for his prey' (*RG* I. ii. 26–7). Surprisingly little attention has been paid to a tantalizingly suggestive reference to Mary Frith herself attending – and *performing* in – *The Roaring Girl*, ironically confirming Sir Alexander's prejudices. According to *The Consistory of London Correction Book*, Frith was

> at a playe about 3 quarters of a yeare since at *the* ffortune in mans apparell & in her boot*es* & with a sword by her syde, she told the company there presen*te tha*t she thought many of them were of opinion *tha*t she was a man, but if any of them would come to her lodging they should finde that she is a woman & some other

immodest & lascivious speaches she also vsed at that time And also sat there vppon the stage in the publique viewe of all the people there presente in mans apparell & playd vppon her lute & sange a songe.⁴¹

Scholars agree the reference is to this play. The extent of her involvement is a matter of speculation, but her presence, in the audience and on stage, raises interesting questions about the play's *collaborative* nature. For *The Roaring Girl* is not only a collaboration between Middleton and Dekker and the Prince's Men who gave it form; it is also a collaborative *event*, bringing into play not only Moll, but Frith also.

*The Consistory of London Correction Book* provides evidence that a woman played a role on a public stage; what *kind* of role will be considered here. The disruption of convention, of all-male acting, is nicely in keeping with a play whose protagonist challenges gender roles, but it begs a number of interesting questions. Was this an impromptu, one-off performance? Was Frith perhaps spotted in the audience (or, as *The Consistory of London Correction Book* may indicate, drew attention to herself), either by playgoers or actors, and prevailed upon to sing '*her* song' in Act IV, Scene i? Editors agree she most likely took the stage at this point, replacing the actor playing Moll.⁴² If this was a one-off, what was her status, as she made her way onto the stage? And, if it became part of the performance, became expected, so that spectators paid to see Frith,⁴³ as the Epilogue may well suggest –

> If what both [writers] have done
> Cannot full pay your expectation,
> The Roaring Girl herself, some few days hence,
> Shall on this stage give larger recompense
>
> (*RG*, Epilogue, ll. 33–6)

– then this 'cameo' (if it is such) would necessarily have had the blessing of the acting company, and perhaps also the dramatists. It would, then, have become a particularly interesting, indeed unprecedented, collaboration.

The moment Frith moves from the yard (or galleries) – unless (and it is a possibility) she is already sitting on the stage – her status changes, and with it our appreciation of the play in performance. As we imagine her offstage, Frith is neither simply a playgoer nor (we may assume for the moment) part of the script. She occupies a liminal space between audience and stage, yet within the gaze, potentially, of all. At the same time, even when unseen, she is vicariously present (albeit 'alter'd') in the representation that is Moll. If Frith's appearance on stage was a one-off, and therefore (presumably) unscripted, we might speculate on the effect it may have had: whether it met with the approval of the playing company, who may have invited her onstage, perhaps flattered by her presence, eager on the spur of the moment to make use of her; or whether perhaps they bowed to the audience's demands. If she appeared regularly, as the Epilogue may suggest, then the acting company (and perhaps, though not necessarily, the dramatists) must have approved, eager to cash in on her notoriety even more. Perhaps, like Moll in the play, Frith provides a successful outcome in the theatre. But, in either case, Frith's presence poses a question mark over the entire play.

*The Roaring Girl* is concerned primarily with appearances, and the gap between signifier and signified. While this is played out in the scenes where men are outwitted precisely because they make erroneous assumptions about Moll, it is, ironically, when Frith enters the playhouse and ascends the stage that the real problems begin. As we have seen, the playwrights seek to challenge the 'common voice': Moll is a chaste, honest figure, 'loose in nothing but in mirth' (*RG* II. ii. 179), who exposes skulduggery wherever she finds it. Playgoers may have found this difficult to accept, or alternatively may have colluded in the romance. But Frith's presence, as she takes *her* place and displaces the actor playing Moll in Act IV, Scene i, must have produced an interesting clash in the playhouse. For, if *The Consistory of London Correction Book* is accurate – and it must be remembered it is a record of a criminal charge rather than an objective account of an event – Frith's performance – and clearly it is such, even before she plays her lute – contrasts starkly with Moll's portrayal. Far from challenging the 'common voice', Frith gives the audience apparently what they want ('lack'), undermining the play's attempt to transform her. It is true that Act IV, Scene i gives Moll a number of double entendres, and her playacting to conform to Sir Alexander's expectations makes Frith's taking the actor's part here, if she did, not inappropriate.

But, combined with her 'immodest and lascivious speeches', this must have jarred with the play's stated aims. Certainly a line such as 'I'll play my part as well as I can' (*RG* IV. i. 85) offers an obvious joke, but at the expense of exposing the play as artifice. The convention that allows theatre to function, what Coleridge called 'the willing suspension of disbelief', is undercut here, and, bearing in mind Frith's celebrity, it is not certain (and we cannot know) whether her appearance was altogether to the play's advantage. Indeed, if women spectators identified with women characters,[44] we may well ask what women in the audience made of this Moll/Frith substitution.

Since critics do not dispute Frith's presence at the Fortune, we can draw two initial conclusions: the playwrights and actors could not entirely control the collaborative material they drew on for their play, nor could they guarantee how audiences would respond. We might ask then whether Frith is a friend or foe to the play. She is certainly a collaborative feature, but welcome or otherwise is not recorded. Nor is it clear, except taking the long view, from the vantage point of an autobiography published after her death, that the play helped Frith herself. For theorists, larger issues are at stake, such as how the play might be read as participating in debates (then and now) on the place of women in early modern society and the possible *frisson* engendered by all-male acting; but it may be useful to view collaboration as a trope that produces a creative, unmanageable friction, so airing concerns that trouble rather than assuage. If Frith is an 'unmasterable excess',[45] it is perhaps the case that it is precisely her presence that gives the play its edge, preventing a romanticized figure from softening the issues raised. For, if neither playwrights nor actors wrote Frith into the play, she is nonetheless there, unscripted, and any consideration of *The Roaring Girl* cannot ignore this collaborative 'shadow'. Arguably it is in the very conjoining of Moll, played by a male actor dressed as a transvestite, and Frith, a transvestite who declares her womanhood, that the collaboration that is *The Roaring Girl* comes to life.

# 4

# Middleton and Shakespeare

While Middleton's and Dekker's collaborations indicate a pattern of allegiances, the plays that associate Middleton with William Shakespeare (1564–1616) suggest a more complex relationship, the precise details and implications of which are far from certain. But it is in the traces of this professional link that we find the most fascinating evidence of the myriad ways in which playwrights worked, and texts were constituted, experienced and reconstituted, in the playhouse. Indeed, in this case particularly, it is a process that continues today in the role scholars, editors, and publishers play in canon formation.

Middleton's connection with Shakespeare is not well known. Yet the surviving evidence indicates that several 'Shakespeare' plays are in fact not his alone, but are linked in various ways to Middleton. As will be shown, these plays reveal – if at the same time obscure – a complex pattern of collaboration. What this pattern indicates challenges long-held assumptions surrounding the consecration of Shakespeare as an independent writer – a writer whose achievement is testament, tradition has it, to individual genius, rather than the product of several hands. This chapter outlines the evidential – and possible – intersections between Middleton and Shakespeare, and focuses on what this 'textual intercourse'[1] might tell us about their collaborative practices.

**PATTERNS**

Unlike Shakespeare, who spent most of his career with one company, Middleton wrote for a number of troupes, adult and child; but, like Shakespeare, Middleton wrote for the King's Men, and this in part explains their connection. One distinct pattern that emerges, then, is directly related to company affiliation. This ought not to surprise us, for clearly it made commercial and artistic sense for writers who worked for the same company to pool or share ideas, and thus make the best use of its resources. Equally, however, playwrights were, of course, competitors (financially) and rivals (artistically), and thus might be considered to be servants of two masters: the company that commissioned them, and their own ambition. It may be useful, then, to think of the various links between Middleton and Shakespeare as being in different degrees materialist and aesthetic.

If the extent of their cooperation remains largely conjectural, they must have thought highly of each other's work, regardless of differences they may have had. As with Dekker, Shakespeare was a writer to whom Middleton turned repeatedly, and this is surely indicative of his respect for the King's Men's principal dramatist. But it is also apparently the case that Shakespeare admired his younger, less-experienced, though proven, contemporary. What is different, however, is the nature of this relationship, for it is one in which the very term 'collaboration' stretches to accommodate the themes identified in this study.

Three 'Shakespeare' plays have been linked with Middleton: *Measure for Measure* (1604), *Timon of Athens* (1605–6) and *Macbeth* (1606); two further King's Men's plays, now attributed to Middleton, may have involved Shakespeare: *A Yorkshire Tragedy* (1605) and *The Lady's Tragedy* (1611).[2] Significantly – a point this chapter will enlarge on – Middleton often alludes to Shakespeare texts. The following discussion makes full use of the definitions of collaboration outlined in Chapter 2, and returns to the theme of intertextuality that this study contends is key to understanding early modern literary production and reception. As will be seen, the moments of intersection that call up Middleton's and Shakespeare's names are often of precisely that kind: *textual*.

**CURRENT SCHOLARSHIP**

The suggestion that Middleton and Shakespeare worked together is not new, but modern editions of 'Shakespeare' plays have tended to play down the association or ignore it altogether. What is emerging, nevertheless, is a growing perception of the likely extent of the relationship, subject as it is to continuing debate, and the light an approach sympathetic to collaboration might shed on the texts, and their making and meaning.

Although the possibility that Shakespeare might not have worked alone was first mooted in the nineteenth century, it is a measure of the hold Shakespeare has that the academy has been slow to register this scholarship. Indeed, only now are plays such as *Titus Andronicus* (1592–3), *Pericles* (1607–8), *Henry VIII* (1613) and *Two Noble Kinsmen* (1613–14) recognized as being collaborations. Yet the history of scholarship documenting Middleton's and Shakespeare's association is surprisingly long established. Shakespeare's sole authorship of *Timon of Athens* was first questioned in 1849 by Charles Knight, and the author of *The Revenger's Tragedy* (then thought to be Cyril Tourneur) was proposed as Shakespeare's collaborator by F. G. Fleay in 1874; Middleton's name finally emerged in an essay by William Wells in 1920.[3] Although Middleton's role in *Timon of Athens* is now accepted, with few exceptions modern editions conceal the fact.[4] Since 1869 it has been recognized that the earliest surviving *Macbeth* (the 1623 folio) includes text that also features in Middleton's *The Witch* (*c*.1616) as well as other, non-Shakespearian material.[5] But editors have tended to play down the significance of this: where these 'interpolations' have been accurately identified, often the purpose has been to delete them from 'Shakespeare's' *Macbeth*, as if to 'return to' a 'Shakespeare original'. The recent Oxford editions[6] are exceptional in restoring Middleton's alterations, thereby recognizing that a *Shakespeare Macbeth* as such simply does not exist, and indeed Middleton's hand is suspected elsewhere in the only surviving, 1623 folio, text. Middleton's role in *Measure for Measure* is a more recent addition to the debate, endorsed by the Oxford editors and discussed at some length.[7] These cases illustrate different forms of what might be understood by the term 'collaboration'.

These three instances alone justify an extended discussion of writing relations between these dramatists. Yet two further plays, both included in the Middleton canon, have also been linked to Shakespeare. *A Yorkshire Tragedy*, attributed to Shakespeare on the 1608 title page and included in the third and fourth folios of 1664 and 1685, is firmly linked to Middleton, either as collaborator[8] or as sole writer.[9] This was one of 'Four Plays in One': the others are lost, so we can only speculate what kind of performance the four plays constituted together, and indeed whether they too were Middleton–Shakespeare collaborations. A still further instance has been suggested recently in the case of *The Lady's Tragedy*, with Shakespeare proposed as the reviser of a text written by his fellow King's Men dramatist,[10] though this has been disputed.[11] Add to these plays a pattern of allusion, echo and intertextuality that connects them through that other collaborative agent, the audience, and the case for an association between Middleton and Shakespeare is irrefutable.

The surviving evidence of this relationship is primarily textual, and secondarily circumstantial. For several plays the evidence is incontrovertible, while for other plays arguments for and against are part of the ongoing debate surrounding the Middleton canon. Whether this leads in time to a reconsideration of the Shakespeare canon remains to be seen. The task here is to examine in detail the extent of their relationship, and explore the theatrical context in which it took place. This retracing not only necessarily embraces overt instances of collaborative writing, varied as these are, but also takes into account intertextual connections. Although not strictly *writers'* collaborations, such echoes and references are nonetheless testament to writers' – and audiences' – knowledge, which collectively constitutes an ongoing playhouse narrative. These instances offer an opportunity to speculate how allusions played, and how they were intended to be read; they may also shed light on the nature of the collaborative relationship itself.

## MIDDLETON, SHAKESPEARE AND THE KING'S MEN

Middleton *may* not have written regularly for the King's Men until around 1614–15,[12] but his association with the company certainly dates from considerably earlier. *The Revenger's Tragedy* was staged in 1606 at the Globe, which had become the King's Men's permanent outdoor venue in 1599, but this was not Middleton's first connection with the company that would perform his sensational political drama *A Game at Chess* in 1624.

We do not know when Middleton and Shakespeare first met, nor would we expect this kind of information to survive. But by dating texts, even approximately, it is possible to construct a general picture. As we have seen, Middleton is first recorded as active in Henslowe's *Diary* in 1602, and, if it is safe to assume he was a regular playgoer, 'daylie accompanynge the players', then he was surely familiar with plays by Shakespeare. Equally, we must assume that Shakespeare knew of Middleton, for several years later the first product of their joint labours was composed. Middleton had a number of starts, in poetry, pamphlets and playwriting. But his association with the King's Men, early, middle and late, with hindsight constitutes the spine of his career.

*Timon of Athens* is an 'orthodox' collaboration – that is, a play written jointly rather than revised later. If it is surprising that an established dramatist should work with a relative novice, the subject of this play clearly suited both writers. *Timon of Athens* anticipates *King Lear* in its treatment of court intrigue and exile, and foreshadows concerns Middleton was to explore throughout his career: how political power is exercised and its effect on the individual, and the centrality of money and desire in social relations. While none of Shakespeare's plays is set in contemporary England, Middleton's early plays, as we have seen, focus on London. *Timon of Athens* draws together two parallel, classical/modern narratives: the phenomenon of the weak ruler and the definition of power in economic terms.

Lear's folly in dividing his kingdom is punished, the state disintegrating into civil war. Like Lear, Timon fails to see through flatterers, but he is nonetheless a sympathetic character who serves a didactic purpose; while Lear's actions are condemned, Timon is the mouthpiece for an overt political critique of his society. In scenes attributed to Middleton a familiar theme emerges: condemnation of a rotten court. The chorus-figure Apemantus comments on Timon's failure to realize that he is surrounded by flatterers, not true friends:

> Hey-day, what a sweep of vanity comes this way!
> They dance? They are madwomen.
> Like madness is the glory of this life
> As this pomp shows to a little oil and root.
> We make ourselves fools to disport ourselves,

> And spend our flatteries to drink those men
> Upon whose age we void it up again
> With poisonous spite and envy.
> Who lives that's not depraved or depraves?
>
> (*TA* I. ii. 124–32)

This portrait anticipates Vindice's commentary in *The Revenger's Tragedy* a year or so later:

> Duke: royal lecher; go, grey-hair'd Adultery;
> And thou his son, as impious steep'd as he;
> And thou his bastard, true-begot in evil;
> And thou his Duchess, that will do with Devil.
> Four ex'lent characters – o that marrowless age
> Would stuff the hollow bones with damn'd desires
> And 'stead of heat kindle infernal fires
> Within the spendthrift veins of a dry Duke,
> A parch'd and juiceless luxur.
>
> (*RT* I. i. 1–9)

If the tone of the two plays is different, we can see already in *Timon of Athens* the theme of court corruption that would become central in Middleton drama. *Timon of Athens* may be regarded as a point of origin for both *King Lear* and *The Revenger's Tragedy*.

Timon's loyal servant Flavius's fears – 'His promises fly so beyond his state|That what he speaks is all in debt, he owes|For every word' (*TA* I. ii. 192–4) – are realized: Timon overreaches himself, and when his debts are called in his 'friends' desert him. In exile Timon condemns the love for gold that has ruined him – perhaps the most overt of Middleton's critiques of society's greed – and, giving him gold, urges Flavius to

> Go, live rich and happy,
> But thus conditioned: thou shalt build from men,
> Hate all, curse all, show charity to none,
> But let the famished flesh slide from the bone
> Ere thou relieve the beggar.
>
> (*TA* IV. iii. 517–21)

The play ends with Timon's death symbolically purging a rotten Athens – a neatly Shakespearian closure that – just perhaps – a Middletonian scepticism undermines. The choice is the audience's.

Further evidence of Middleton's association with the King's Men during this period is suggested in *The Revenger's Tragedy*, whose revengeful, illegitimate character Spurio recalls *King Lear*'s Edmund. Here again, court corruption links the plays. Disenfranchised, Edmund rails against his father's disdain for him, which the audience has witnessed in the opening scene:

> Thou, nature, art my goddess. To thy law
> My services are bound.
> . . . . .
>       Why 'bastard'? Wherefore 'base',
> When my dimensions are as well compact,
> My mind as generous, and my shape as true
> As honest madam's issue?
> . . . . .
> Legitimate Edgar, I must have your land.
> Our father's love is to the bastard Edmund
> As to the legitimate. Well, my legitimate, if
> This letter speed and my invention thrive,
> Edmund the base shall to th' legitimate.
> I grow, I prosper. Now gods, stand up for bastards!
>       (*KL* 1608 Quarto, II. 1–2, 6–9, 16–21)

In *The Revenger's Tragedy* Spurio similarly justifies nature's role in forming his character:

> Duke, thou didst do me wrong, and by thy act
> Adultery is my nature.
> Faith, if the truth were known, I was begot
> After some gluttonous dinner, some stirring dish
> Was my first father, when deep healths went round,
> And ladies' cheeks were painted red with wine,
> . . . . .
> As for my brother, the Duke's only son,
> Whose birth is more beholding to report
> Than mine, and yet perhaps as falsely sown
> (Women must not be trusted with their own),
> I'll loose my days upon him, hate all I;
> Duke, on thy brow I'll draw my bastardy.
> For indeed a bastard by nature should make cuckolds
> Because he is the son of a cuckold-maker.
>       (*RT* I. ii. 176–81, 195–202)

This kind of parallelism reveals not only the company-mediated intertextuality with which we are familiar, and which playgoers at the Globe in 1606 may have appreciated, but invites questions about the precise *performance* of such moments in the playhouse. Both *King Lear* and *The Revenger's Tragedy* are concerned with the struggle between age and youth, a common theme both playwrights employed. There is no clear sign that Middleton subverts Edmund's speech in this 'quotation', but it has been suggested that his later, collaborative play *The Old Law* (1618) 'is a comic rendering of the struggle depicted in *Lear*'.[13] As we will see, Middleton–Shakespeare collaborations, in all their forms, are complex and plural, complicating the scholar's desire to retrace the playwrights' footsteps and make sense of what the surviving textual evidence might tell us. But what stands out and demands our attention is Middleton's visiting and revisiting of texts, offering new interpretations of old material.

With *Macbeth* this becomes especially pertinent. While *Timon of Athens* was jointly written, the provenance of *Macbeth* is rather more complicated. The undisputed facts are these. *Macbeth* features material that is also present in *The Witch*. What is not straightforward is the relationship between the two plays, and how they came to be connected. While this is a 'textual' matter, it is also of interest because how this link is interpreted has a direct bearing on our understanding of the playwrights' relationship. Both plays exploited a fascination for witchcraft that James's accession in 1603 had stimulated. The King took a personal interest in the subject, believing it to be a potent force that threatened rulers: in 1597 he had published *Demonology* to repudiate Reginald Scot's *Discovery of Witchcraft* (1584); in 1603 *Demonology* was republished, and Scot's sceptical treatise banned. When the King's Men performed *Macbeth*, it might reasonably be assumed that the play endorsed James's beliefs, especially since Shakespeare's version contradicts Holinshed by stressing that James's supposed ancestor, Banquo, had no role in the murder of Duncan, the legitimate king. The witches' role is to encourage Macbeth to yield to ambition and overthrow his king. The play begins with the witches introducing confusion – 'When the battle's lost, and won' (*M*. I. i. 4); 'Fair is foul, and foul is fair' (*M*. I. i. 10) – which Macbeth's first line echoes: 'So foul and fair a day I have not seen' (*M*. I. iii. 36). Macbeth's overthrow of Duncan is due to the witches' influence, confirming for believers the potency of witchcraft; Macbeth's death is symbolically a defeat of sorcery and restoration of legitimate rule.

To *Macbeth* Middleton added two 'witch scenes', the whole of Act III, Scene v, and much of Act IV, Scene i; both plays feature two songs, though the 1623 folio did not include them in full,[14] and share in Hecate a particularly 'theatrical' witch. The effect of these additions is to accentuate the role of witchcraft in *Macbeth*. Three key issues arise: the dating of the plays; the possible rationale for Middleton's changes to *Macbeth*; and what this might tell us about the revision of scripts for the King's Men – and the relationship between Middleton and Shakespeare.

There is no doubt that *Macbeth* is the earlier play; although the date of *The Witch* is uncertain, it cannot be earlier than 1609, and is probably not later than 1616. So the question that arises initially is when the additions were made – and whether they antedate or postdate *The Witch*. Two possibilities arise. Middleton's description of the play in his Dedication as 'ignorantly ill-fated' was long believed to indicate *The Witch* had failed on the stage, but critics argue that Middleton was referring to a political controversy, suggesting the play failed for other than aesthetic reasons.[15] Middleton, the argument goes, added elements from *The Witch* to the King's Men's revival of *Macbeth*, presumably to refloat his political critique. Alternatively, *Macbeth* was revised by Middleton in 1609–10, the Hecate scenes being added at this point and then reused in *The Witch*, written several years later.[16] Middleton frequently returns to both his own and others' texts, so this kind of appropriation should not surprise us. Whatever the order of events, the links between the two plays invite speculation about how this intersection might be read.

A clear opposition arises – at least as a critical proposition. If *Macbeth* supports belief in the existence of witches, *The Witch* is altogether more sceptical. If, then, *Macbeth* apparently endorsed King James's beliefs (and fears), *The Witch*, drawing heavily on the critique by Scot that James sought to refute,[17] may be read as seeking to undermine the popular superstition that witches were behind evil acts. Macbeth is inspired by witches who urge him to fulfil the prophecy 'that [he] shalt be king hereafter!' (*M.* I. iii. 48). In *The Witch* it is made clear that the forces of evil lie not in old women mixing potions but in the court itself: the rottenness of the state is not to be explained by condemning the vulnerable women who, Scot had pointed out, are accused of witchcraft to explain disasters, but exposed from within. Middleton's witches verge on caricature, exaggerating popular fears in a burlesque that strains credibility – intentionally.

Recent scholarship, identifying Middleton as an overtly political dramatist, finds *The Witch* was written in response to a spectacular, contemporary political crisis that went to the heart of James's court – the Frances Carr scandal discussed in the opening chapter of this study. The divorce in 1613 and murder trials in 1615–16 signal both the public markers of the scandal and the range of likely dates of performance, and thus may determine the parameters of a play whose political and theatrical coordinates remain open to question. If, as Brooke argues, Middleton revised *Macbeth* and then wrote *The Witch* several years later, then one conclusion, impossible to prove, is irresistible: Shakespeare agreed to the changes made by his collaborator. Shakespeare was active until as late as 1614: it is perhaps unlikely changes were made to *Macbeth* without his knowledge and, possibly, approval. If, however, Middleton first wrote *The Witch* and then, in the face of political problems, revised *Macbeth*, adding the Scot-derived critique of witchcraft material from *The Witch*, then the folio *Macbeth* is a different kind of collaboration. In this scenario, Shakespeare and Middleton conceived different *Macbeths*. Perhaps Middleton implicitly critiques Shakespeare's play; or, alternatively, he regarded *Macbeth* as an ideal vehicle for material from *The Witch*; or, the King's Men approached Middleton to revise the old play and 'spice it up' a bit. It may be that there are elements of all three possibilities. What we do know is that, when Shakespeare's former colleagues came to assemble the folio, they considered *Macbeth*, with Middleton's additions, to be a 'Shakespeare' play.

The dating of the revision of *Macbeth* and the composition of *The Witch* are irresolvable, unless further evidence is found. But the debate and its implications are interesting for another reason. The opposed readings, leading to different conclusions, in turn offer two possibilities that pivot on whether Middleton and Shakespeare are considered collaborators or competitors. Yet the implied opposition, *The Witch* v. *Macbeth*, is perhaps more a scholar's sleight of hand than an accurate reading of events. As two recent studies suggest, witchcraft was associated with the Gunpowder Plot of 1605 and subsequent fears of Catholic outrages, for it was popularly believed that the 1615–16 revelations had uncovered a plot as serious as that of 1605.[18] Both plays may be regarded as tapping into this climate of fear; similarly both playwrights, perhaps for different reasons, sought to make political points through their exploration of the contemporary meanings of witchcraft. It is conceivable that Middleton made additions to *Macbeth* around 1615–16 on the grounds that it would not have had to be run past the censor again: *The Witch* and the revised *Macbeth* may in fact have been very close in time.

With the third of these texts the question of date and provenance has been established with a much greater degree of certainty. *Measure for Measure* was definitely a 'posthumous collaboration': when Middleton revised the play Shakespeare was dead. Middleton reworked *Measure for Measure* in late 1621, adding material that emphasized what scholars recognize to be Middleton's Protestant politics.[19] Although *Measure for Measure* is not a joint collaboration as such, its provenance as a King's Men's play justifies its inclusion in the present discussion, for like *Macbeth* it exists only in the 1623 folio. It is once again important to remember in a case such as this that texts belonged to companies, not to dramatists: Middleton's revision of *Measure for Measure* was then a company matter, even if his revisions were politically motivated. (Middleton's possible revision of Fletcher's *The Nice Valour* in 1622, probably also for the King's Men, may be another example of such political rewriting.) In *The Phoenix* (like *Measure for Measure* a 1604 play) Middleton had dramatized a similar theme: a ruler in disguise who spies on his subjects; *Measure for Measure* afforded Middleton an opportunity to revisit this topic for the King's Men. As with *Macbeth*, Middleton drew on a play through which he could convey his political views. Just as *Macbeth* may have had a new political meaning in *c.*1616, *Measure for Measure* in 1621 was a different play, in the collaborative environment of the playhouse, than it had been in 1604. If early in the century the play articulated the optimism and hopes many had for the new reign, by 1621 the play had changed, the duke taking on a much more sinister appearance, reflecting the disillusion, and disappointment, many now felt. Tellingly, his disguise as a friar now took on an added significance. Coming at the height of the crisis over the Spanish match, Middleton's revision of *Measure for Measure* is a fascinating example of how a text takes on a markedly different hue when its context changes. In *Macbeth* and *Measure for Measure* Middleton demonstrates a knack for a particularly nuanced kind of adaptation, a knack to which the compilers of the 1623 Folio seem to have given their approval.

Middleton certainly revised plays by Shakespeare; it may be that Shakespeare similarly mediated a play written by his colleague. Until recently *The Lady's Tragedy* was known as *The Second Maiden's Tragedy*, a title bestowed by the Master of the Revels, Sir George Buc, who licensed the play on 31 October 1611.[20] His intervention neatly suggests that the Master of the Revels was at once a censor *and* a collaborator in the allowing and making of plays, but more intriguing is the role Shakespeare may have played. Fortunately for scholars the company's manuscript promptbook, with Buc's emendations, has survived, but the evidence is open to a number of interpretations. Before issuing the licence, Buc demanded a number of changes, sending the play back to the King's Men to be altered. This raises an interesting question: *who* made the changes – were they *authorial* (that is, by Middleton), or is *The Lady's Tragedy* an example of *playhouse* revision? Shakespeare has been proposed as reviser,[21] though this has been challenged;[22] what is apparent is that *The Lady's Tragedy* echoes several Shakespeare plays – which ought not to surprise students of Middleton. Perhaps, alternatively or additionally, Shakespeare had a hand in the play after it left the censor and came back to the company.

*The Lady's Tragedy* deploys familiar Middleton material – a court ruled by tyranny, desire and deception. To take several related examples of the enforced changes made by the King's Men: Buc objected to the lines 'I must put on|a Courtiers face'; in its place the reviser(s) substituted 'I must put on|a brazen face';[23] similarly, 'courtier girl' is crossed out and the reviser has inserted 'woman', while 'I would not trust at court and [if] I could choose' becomes 'I would not trust but few'.[24] Like *The Revenger's Tragedy* and *The Witch* (and *Macbeth*), the play clearly alludes – *too* clearly – to contemporary concerns directly or tangentially associated with James's court. It appears that Buc excised a transparent reference to the murder of King Henri IV in 1610, an event that had so appalled James, 'Frenchmens' becoming 'extremest', while again the spectre of the Essex–Howard marriage may have alerted him: he owed his position to Lady Frances's family, and his sensitivity to elements of the play is suggested in the cuts he demanded.[25] But, like all interpreters, Buc saw some things and apparently missed others: the play could also be read as alluding to the imprisonment of Arbella Stuart and William Seymour, who had angered James by marrying in secret, yet this material was not censored. Unlike *The Witch* – and like *Macbeth* – *The Lady's Tragedy* proved adaptable to register current affairs, despite suffering the attentions of the censor. Whoever revised the play, the King's Men were left with a text that played to contemporary concerns – and accommodated Middleton's politics. Whether or not Shakespeare was directly or indirectly involved in the (re)writing of *The Lady's Tragedy*, 'Shakespeare' is detectable in the extant text, as 'he' is, most strikingly, in what is surely Middleton's greatest 'anti-court' drama. Indeed, as the concept 'audience collaboration' stretches to realize the Barthesian shift from 'author' to 'reader', it is in *The Revenger's Tragedy* that a Middleton–Shakespeare association is most transparent.

## MIDDLETON AND *HAMLET*

Early modern drama is self-reflexive, evoking moments from earlier plays that then live on, albeit changed, for later playgoers. Recalled in performance as well as in the memory, plays enjoyed afterlives in quotation, visual and verbal echoes blending older moments into new contexts. These allusions invite a double reading, for they are potentially both imitative and parodic. If such echoes can tell us much about the popularity of plays and audience tastes, they may also reveal something of the artistic relations between dramatists. As the final chapter of this study shows, Middleton frequently returns to his own work. It should not surprise us then that a dramatist who collaborated throughout his career also recalled plays by others. The intertextual links between Middleton and Shakespeare are particularly interesting. That these echoes are chiefly in one direction – Middleton alluding to Shakespeare – might confirm the orthodox view that ranks Shakespeare so much higher than his contemporaries. But, just as the interpretative possibilities surrounding the provenance of *Macbeth* and its relationship with *The Witch* make firm conclusions impossible, these intertextual connections invite a number of readings. That they occurred both during and after their joint work for the King's Men makes this feature of Middleton's career particularly intriguing.

Middleton's intertextual relations with Shakespeare span his entire career. In *The Ghost of Lucrece* (1600) Middleton echoes but departs from Shakespeare's *The Rape of Lucrece*, published six years previously,[26] and as late as *The Changeling* (1622) evoked one of the stage's best-known villains, De Flores calling up memories of *Richard III*.[27] The Lucrece poems will be considered in greater detail in the final chapter; here the focus is on Middleton's reworking of one of Shakespeare's most famous plays. The overlap between collaborative and allusive work is indicative not only of the professional and artistic closeness of these writers, but also of the interconnections between their collaborative work and Middleton's reading of Shakespeare.

Middleton turned to *Hamlet* in several plays, most obviously in *The Revenger's Tragedy*. *Hamlet* dramatizes the protagonist's quest for justice, but Hamlet's inability for much of the play to act on his suspicions allows the playwright to explore the ethics of revenge and the limits of knowledge, the prince musing that 'conscience does make cowards of us all' (*H.* III. i. 85). *The Revenger's Tragedy* may be regarded as a spectacularly *theatrical* rewriting of Shakespeare's play, and its protagonist, whose name means 'revenger', read as a parodic Hamlet consumed by bloodlust, not doubt. In the opening scene Vindice evokes that most poignant of moments, Hamlet's 'Alas poor Yorick' speech (*H.* V. i. 171.ff):

> [*To the skull.*] Thou sallow picture of my poison'd love,
> My study's ornament, thou shell of death,
> Once the bright face of my betrothed lady,
> When life and beauty naturally fill'd out
> These ragged imperfections,
> When two heaven-pointed diamonds were set
> In those unsightly rings – then 'twas a face
>
> (*RT* I. i. 14–20)

It is as if Hamlet has jumped into Ophelia's grave and Vindice emerged, clutching the skull. Middleton's revenger carries about him the skull of his beloved, by 'The old Duke poison'd, | Because thy purer part would not consent | Unto his palsy-lust' (*RT* I. i. 32–4), as a *memento mori*, or remembrance of death. This macabre object is not only a spur to revenge, however, but a theatrical prop that will itself play a role in avenging its own death (a moment echoed in turn in *The Lady's Tragedy*).

This palimpsest is underscored further if Richard Burbage, the King's Men's most famous actor, played Vindice after taking the role of Hamlet,[28] and the treatment of revenge, court corruption and incest all point to an explicit rewriting. Indeed, the use of Gloriana's skull to fashion 'the bony lady' (*RT* III. vi. 120), whose poisoned lips will kill her killer the Duke, neatly collapse the play's dual concerns, sex and death, evoking the early modern meaning of 'to die' as both literal and metaphorical, actual death and the bliss of orgasm. Middleton works into (and out of) *Hamlet* the materialist implications of desire, broadening out Hamlet's fear of madness into Vindice's manic yet irresistibly logical conclusion that 'Surely we are all mad people' (*RT* III. v. 79). Vindice goes to his death not fearing what is to come but, Hamlet-like, concerned that the 'story' be told: 'This murder might have slept in tongueless brass, | But for ourselves, and the world died an ass' (*RT* V. iii. 113–14).

Yet it would be misleading to suggest that Middleton simply parodies *Hamlet*. Certain oppositions can be proposed – for example, *Hamlet* as concerned with the weight of the past, while *The Revenger's Tragedy* focuses on the present, and the desire for revenge;[29] and, of course, the protagonists are very different, though hardly polar opposites – too much can be made of Hamlet's delay, at the risk of ignoring his ruthlessness. But the thematic correspondences suggest continuity as much as difference, and it is worth pointing out that in a specific theatrical and cultural sense *Hamlet* lives on through and during *The Revenger's Tragedy*. If Gloriana's skull recalls Yorick's, Vindice does not contradict Hamlet's musing on death and remembrance – 'Here hung those lips that I have kissed I know not how oft' (*H.* V. i. 174–5); the difference lies in the later play's conscious theatricality. If *The Revenger's Tragedy* mocks Hamlet's failure to enact his revenge, it does not necessarily mock *Hamlet* the play.

That *Hamlet* is a rich source for Middleton is clear from the echoes in three later plays, *A Fair Quarrel* (with Rowley, 1616), *More Dissemblers Besides Women* (1614), and *Hengist, King of Kent* (1620). In what has been described as the play's 'dialogue with *Hamlet*',[30] *A Fair Quarrel*'s dramatization of a contemporary controversy, the rights and wrongs of duelling, offers a theatrical palimpsest that replays Hamlet, Gertrude and Laertes through Captain Ager, his mother and the Colonel. Ager's defence of his mother's honour – the colonel calls him 'son of a whore' – becomes a quest for knowledge, here of her claim to chastity, a familiar Middleton theme. In what critics have identified as a Middleton trademark, an unlikely or implausible resolution to events drawing attention to the absurdity of social (and perhaps dramatic) convention, *A Fair Quarrel* resolves matters with artifice. Inga-Stina Ewbank also suggests that *More Dissemblers Besides Women* echoes *Hamlet*; the possibility that Burbage played a leading role here too allows the critic to speculate about a further level of intertextuality.[31]

This '*Hamlet* narrative' is clearly evident in *Hengist, King of Kent*, where the verbal echo is unmistakable. Polonius's famous lines announcing the players –

> The best actors in the world, either for tragedy, comedy, history, pastoral, pastorical-comical, historical-pastoral, tragical-historical, tragical-comical-historical-pastoral, scene individable, or poem unlimited.

> (H. II. ii. 379–82)

is replayed in the arrival of a troupe of players in *Hengist, King of Kent*:

> SYMON. [N]ow sirs are yow Commedians[?]
> 2 CHEATER. [W]e are any thing Sir: Commedians, Tragedians, Tragicommedians, Cometragedians, pastorilists, humerists, Clownists, and saterists, we haue em sir, from the smile to the laugh; from the laugh to the handcercheife.

> (HKK 2316–23)

Simon's remark that 'a play may be dangerous, | I haue knowne a greate man poysoned in a play' (*HKK* 2401–2) may well refer to *The Murder of Gonzago* in *Hamlet*, and the Polonius reference is unmistakable. That the usurper Vortiger in *Hengist, King of Kent* also echoes *Richard III* is further evidence of a Middleton–Shakespeare intertextual link.

What is particularly interesting about these plays is that they were all performed at the Globe by the King's Men, the company for whom Middleton wrote extensively from around the time of Shakespeare's retirement. This adds a further level to the issue of intertextuality, for it raises the possibility not only of a specific audience, and a knowledgeable auditory, but also of actors giving 'repeat' performances in different roles, thus availing spectators of a complex intertexuality in the performer himself. It is impossible to trace the figure – or *actor* – of Burbage through these plays, for the evidence has simply not survived; but such a possibility sets up interesting performative and interpretative dynamics. What it also does is suggest that to posit an antagonistic relationship between Middleton and Shakespeare is not only to ignore their collaborative work but also to miss the subtle, complex and plural moments of theatre that call up a memory of an older play, and fuse it into the present.

## MIDDLETON V. SHAKESPEARE?

The links between Middleton and Shakespeare, varied as they are, throw up a number of questions. Knowledge of their collaborations ought, eventually, to influence editors; and the intertextual echoes, together with the recognition that Middleton appears to have worked extensively for the King's Men, suggest that our understanding of Middleton, and of Middleton and Shakespeare, needs to be re-examined.

Modern criticism, inevitably, has measured early modern dramatists against their contemporary, Shakespeare, or, more accurately, against the academy's Shakespeare. Critics who praise Middleton have tended, like Eliot, to claim that he is second only to Shakespeare.[32] More recently, however, Middleton has been proposed as an *alternative* to Shakespeare. In an important essay Gary Taylor argues that Shakespeare's cultural centrality neuters his political power, whereas Middleton's modern renaissance makes it possible for his politics *then* to be re-experienced now, anew:[33] Middleton was and is a politically oppositional writer, while Shakespeare's oppositional status as a writer with Catholic sympathies has long since been appropriated by the cultural apparatus of the modern state – the academy, theatre and schools.

Whether Middleton will emerge as a radical alternative remains to be seen, but what Taylor's essay highlights is another opposition, between 'then' and 'now', how historicizing the past is also a reading of the past through the present. Thus attempts to think 'purely' in terms of early modern conditions of production so as to arrive at a sense of the context in which writers worked inevitably encounter a modern bias that has already made value judgements about plays and playwrights. Paradoxically, then, a study such as this cannot avoid the gravitational pull that is Shakespeare, for in the wake of Middleton's 'rise' comes the figure of Shakespeare himself.

If for some critics Middleton is a 'radical alternative' – then and now – his collaboration with Shakespeare poses a number of questions. Taylor contends that they were both writing 'opposition' drama, though from different perspectives, one probably Catholic, the other certainly Protestant, both suspicious and critical of the state. No evidence has survived to indicate that they liked or disliked each other. They may have been brought together by the King's Men, but as a sharer and an established playwright it is unlikely Shakespeare collaborated unwillingly. Positing an opposition between them is then a matter for the academy rather than the historian, and it is an opposition the evidence of their collaborations complicates.

And yet there is, too, ample evidence to sketch a scene in which the subversive Middleton undermines the conservative Shakespeare. The echoes of *Hamlet* may mock, and not merely to gratify a knowledgeable auditory; and the 'bewitching' of *Macbeth* offers the modern reader a modern Middleton who, sceptical of the existence of witchcraft and alert to double-dealing at court, subverts Shakespeare's attempt to flatter his company's patron, if such it was. It is arguable that Middleton's revisions of *Measure for Measure* and *Macbeth* offered – through rewriting – a radically different perspective on James from the one the plays presented in the early years of his reign. Though both are 'Shakespeare' plays – consecrated as such by his literary executors, the editors of the first folio – in these two plays Middleton and Shakespeare are bound together, as the collaborators they were. Above all, however, all the examples traced in this chapter illustrate the plural and complex meanings texts made available to playgoers and playwrights alike.

# 5

# Middleton and Rowley

The collaboration between Middleton and Rowley was one of the most successful of the period, and produced one of its finest plays, *The Changeling* (1622). The quality of their collaboration has been acknowledged by a number of critics. R. H. Barker notes that *A Fair Quarrel* (1616) and *The Changeling*, both written with Rowley, have a directness and conciseness unsurpassed in Middleton's other work.[1] R. V. Holdsworth writes of 'Middleton and Rowley's unique success as a collaborating team'.[2] Not surprisingly therefore it has attracted some interesting discussions of the collaborative process.

In addition to *The Changeling*, they wrote *Wit at Several Weapons* (1613), *A Fair Quarrel*, *The Old Law* (1618) and *The World Tossed at Tennis* (1620). Of these the attribution of the first is complicated by the fact that it appears in the Beaumont and Fletcher Folio of 1647, but linguistic analysis appears to confirm it was written by Middleton and Rowley.[3] *The Old Law* was attributed to Massinger, Middleton and Rowley in the first printed edition of 1656, and there has been much discussion of Massinger, possibly as a reviser. Catherine Shaw concurs with Barker that there is little evidence to suggest that Massinger had any definite part in the writing of *The Old Law*,[4] while Lake agrees that the play is almost entirely by Middleton and Rowley, with the possibility that a few lines are by Massinger or an 'unknown dramatist'.[5] The Oxford Middleton proposes the presence of Thomas Heywood. One other play, *The Spanish Gypsy* (1623), has been attributed to Middleton and Rowley, based on the title page of the first edition of 1653. It has been the subject of some discussion: Dekker's and Ford's names have been linked with it, and Lake admits the possibility that these two dramatists may have been revisers of an earlier Middleton

73

and Rowley play. It is included in the Oxford edition and attributed to all four writers.

## WILLIAM ROWLEY

Information about Rowley is sparse. His date of birth is uncertain, probably *c.*1585; he died in 1626. Most of what is known comes from theatrical records. His name is associated with those of John Day and George Wilkins and *The Travels of Three Brothers* (1607), a play presented by Queen Anne's Men. However, from at least 1609 until 1623 he was writing for and acting with the Duke of York's, later Prince Charles's Men, becoming leader of the company in 1616. For the last years of his life he was attached to the King's Men. Most of Rowley's dramatic work was done as a collaborator: only two or three plays are thought to be his unaided work. Until recently he has often been regarded as a collaborating hack, but his connection with plays such as *The Witch of Edmonton* (1621, with Dekker and Ford), and particularly *A Fair Quarrel* and *The Changeling*, indicates that he deserves more serious consideration. The fact that as accomplished a dramatist as Middleton worked quite extensively with Rowley, and probably wrote parts for him (Plumporridge in *The Inner Temple Masque* (1619), and the Fat Bishop in *A Game at Chess* (1624)), suggests respect for the man as a writer and an actor. Rowley was the Prince's Men's leading comic actor, and it was, perhaps, his experience as a performer that enabled him to contribute significantly, particularly as a writer of comic scenes. Certainly it was his practice in his own plays to write a part for himself: with Middleton he wrote, and played, the part of Simplicity in *The World Tossed at Tennis*, and it is likely he played Chough in *A Fair Quarrel*, Gnotho in *The Old Law* and Lollio in *The Changeling*. What should give Rowley's detractors pause for thought is the fact that linguistic analysis shows Rowley contributed more scenes than Middleton, and not exclusively the comic plots, but also the important opening and closing scenes in these three plays. At the same time, the view that collaboration always involved individual dramatists simply writing different parts of the play is no longer tenable, and Michael E. Mooney and Richard L. Nochimson challenge this assumption.[6]

## THE COLLABORATIVE PROCESS

Mooney accepts the well-established view that Rowley wrote the first and last acts and the comic subplots while Middleton wrote the main plot scenes in Acts II, III and IV, in both *A Fair Quarrel* and *The Changeling*. This collaborative technique he calls 'framing'. He goes on to make the assumption that they then made a final revision together to bring the plays into their final shape. He assumes, like R. V. Holdsworth, that the division of labour put to best use the individual abilities of the two dramatists, with Rowley as comic actor writing the comic subplots.[7] However, Middleton had had extensive experience as a writer of comedy and obviously had the ability to write comic plots. Nochimson, while partially accepting Mooney's analysis of *The Changeling*, suggests that the two playwrights actually worked much more closely together to produce a unified and coherent play. The linguistic analyses of Lake and Jackson have served to support and provide evidence for earlier assumptions about the authorship of individual scenes, but they cannot be accepted unreservedly as necessarily indicative of the complete process of collaboration. Indeed, the assumptions behind such analyses are open to question, as 'accommodation theory' suggests. Charles Cathcart points out that 'the process of collaboration may encourage writers to adapt not only their subject-matter and choice of expression, but the very use of colloquialism, contractions, and functional vocabulary that supposedly gives a distinctive imprint to their writing'.[8]

Given the problems and uncertainties of tracing the practice of collaboration, this chapter will look not at the division of labour between writers but how collaborative texts work as performance texts, and examine the qualities that are distinctive of Middleton and Rowley's collaboration.

## THE PLAYS

One of the formal features of *A Fair Quarrel*, *The Old Law* and *The Changeling* is their alternation between comic and tragic modes, and, indeed, the first two may be described as tragicomedies. *The Changeling* has some similar features but is clearly a tragedy, with deaths on stage (not averted, as in tragicomedy). Yet the conclusion of the play is rather unlike most tragedies of the period. An audience might have expected Alsemero's reply to Vermandero's despairing cry, immediately after the death of Beatrice-Joanna, 'Oh, my name is enter'd now in that record | Where till this fatal hour 'twas never read' (*C.* V. iii. 180–1), to be followed by the final four lines of the scene thus:

> ALSEMERO. Let it be blotted out, let your heart lose it,
> And it can never look you in the face,
> Nor tell a tale behind the back of life
> To your dishonour; justice hath so right
> The guilty hit, that innocence is quit
> By proclamation, and may joy again.
>
> (*C.* V. iii. 182–7)

followed by

> Sir, you have yet a son's duty living,
> Please you accept it; let that your sorrow,
> As it goes from your eye, go from your heart;
> Man and his sorrow at the grave must part.
>
> (*C.* V. iii. 215–18)

Such would have preserved a recognizably tragic mood, but between these two speeches the dramatists insert nearly twenty lines of dialogue, cataloguing all the changes that have occurred: the transformation of Beatrice-Joanna, Alsemero's own experience of change, that of Tomazo, down through the social levels of the play, from Antonio and Franciscus, to Isabella and Alibius, modulating the mood towards that of comedy. At the end of this sequence, Alibius, like the jealous husband at the end of so many comedies, acknowledges his foolishness and vows he will change into a better husband. It is only then that Alsemero's final four lines restore the tone of tragedy: 'Man and his sorrow at the grave must part.' After the preceding passionate psychological intensity and complexity the sequence seems almost jaunty and playful, even superficial. Comic and tragic elements of the play are brought together at this point, providing alternative perspectives. Even the Epilogue, which seems to be directing us back towards tragedy – 'All we can do to comfort one another' (*C.* V. iii. 219) – moves from talk of tears to talk of smiles, and concludes 'all griefs are reconcil'd' (*C.* V. iii. 226).

This switching between comic and tragic modes, indeed the coexistence of alternative or comparative perspectives, is also a central feature of *The Old Law*. The Duke reveals that the law requiring the execution of elderly people, promulgated at the beginning of the play, has been a device to test his courtiers, and that all the elders, whom everyone had thought dead, are alive. To the sound of solemn music they appear. The tragicomic ending seems to be complete when the ruler elevates Cleanthes and Hippolita as moral examples and arbiters of filial and matrimonial behaviour. However, suddenly the sound of fiddle music is heard and Gnotho appears, leading a procession in which those at the front are full of jollity for his wedding to young Siren, while those at the back are full of sorrow for Agatha, his old wife, whom he is taking to execution. The dignified and satisfying tragicomic resolution towards which the play seemed to be moving with the revelation that the elders are alive is suddenly disturbed, and the scene shifts again towards comedy. The following sequence shows that, whatever the neatness and justice of Evander's plan, in the real world the passing and cancelling of laws leads only to confusion amongst his subjects. Gnotho turns to the Duke just before he leaves, saying 'Heaven bless and mend your laws that they do not gull your poor countrymen' (*OL* V. i. 595–6). A short sequence follows in which Creon addresses his servants, modulating the scene back towards a serious mood. When only the courtiers remain on stage, Evander moves the scene towards final judgment and tragicomic closure.

This shift in mood challenges the audience to reassess and reconsider assumptions, and is characteristic of many Middleton plays, most noticeably his collaborations with Rowley. Mooney's observation that in *The Changeling* the comic scenes clarify what is implied in the other plot, and that the alternation of paired sets of scenes stresses their interrelationship, identifies distinctive features of Middleton and Rowley collaborations: the clarity of plotting and the ways the different plots are used in relation to each other to develop and illuminate themes. In this respect, there is a marked difference between these plays and *The Witch* or *More Dissemblers Besides Women*, for example, written in the same phase of Middleton's career.

*A Fair Quarrel* is centred round the concept of honour. When the Colonel calls Captain Ager the 'son of a whore' Ager does not immediately challenge him to a duel but questions his mother, who is, unsurprisingly, deeply shocked and insulted. But when her son goes to fight she pretends that the false charge is actually accurate to prevent her son endangering his life. Ager withdraws, only for the Colonel to charge him with cowardice, which gives him just cause to fight the duel. The second plot is the familiar New Comedy-derived model: young lovers, Jane and Fitzallen, desire to marry but are opposed by her father, Russell, who has chosen Chough for her husband. In *A Fair Quarrel* a high degree of integral consistency and cohesion is achieved with the two plots neatly linked through the Colonel's kinship with Fitzallen, and Lady Ager's with Russell. In the first scene, the Colonel's insulting reference to Ager as the son of a whore, which sets off the action of the first plot, arises out of kinship loyalties: the Colonel's reaction to Russell's refusal to save Fitzallen from prison, and Ager's defence of his uncle's stance. The clown scenes are linked to the second plot, as Chough, who attends the roaring school, is the husband Russell has chosen for Jane. Although the two long clown scenes may seem at first to stand out separately from the other material, they provide a parody of the concern in both plots with codes and concepts of honour. In particular the roaring school parallels the duelling code of Ager and the Colonel, with slanging matches between opponents in which catchwords and phrases are repeated, becoming running gags. The abuse is full of sexual suggestion and involves impugning the reputation of the opponent's sister, thus paralleling the concern with female honour in relation both to Lady Ager and to Jane. The ridiculous nature of roaring thus reflects back on to duelling and ideas of honour, exposing them to question and mockery, a theme Middleton had earlier explored with Dekker in *The Roaring Girl*.

Most critical attention has been paid to the relationship and scenes between Captain Ager and his mother, and they are indeed full of psychological interest and dramatic reversals. In this respect they bear some relation to Vindice's testing of his mother and sister in *The Revenger's Tragedy*. However, this focus on the first plot has tended to draw attention away from the second. At first it appears to be a standard New Comedy situation of young lovers whose path to happiness is blocked by a father who wants his daughter to marry a rich man she does not love. What makes it different is that Jane is pregnant and is being blackmailed by the Physician from whom she has sought help. The situation is darker and more serious than those of many New Comedy plots, and Act III, Scene ii looks forward to the desperate scene between Beatrice-Joanna and De Flores in *The Changeling*. Jane wants to show gratitude for the Physician's help by giving him money, but, like De Flores, he scorns pecuniary reward; he holds power over her because he knows her secret, attempts to kiss her and demands sexual gratification as payment. The lines that precede his attempt to kiss Jane are transformed in *The Changeling* into that powerful utterance of De Flores, 'Y'are the deed's creature' (C. III. iv. 137):

| | |
|---|---|
| PHYSICIAN. | . . . indeed I love you. |
| JANE. | In deed? what deed? |
| PHYSICIAN. | The deed that you have done. |
| JANE. | I cannot believe you. |
| PHYSICIAN. | Believe the deed then. |
| | [*Offers to kiss her*] |
| | (*FQ* III. ii. 97–9) |

Here is the germ of the idea for that famous scene in the later play: the secret, the offering and rejection of money, the physical assault, the sexual demand and the emphasis upon 'the deed'. It is interesting to reflect that, according to most attribution studies, Rowley is credited with the scene in *A Fair Quarrel* and Middleton with the scene in *The Changeling*. This is surely an example of the complex ways collaboration worked, and a further indication that it is simplistic to suggest that one dramatist wrote a particular scene within a collaborative work as if the other had no input at all.

*The Old Law* displays a similar narrative clarity and interrelation of plots. The law encourages young men, like Simonides, to bring elderly parents to execution, and young wives, like Eugenia, with elderly husbands to anticipate their demise by encouraging the attentions of young courtiers, while Gnotho goes about to falsify the parish records in order to get rid of his wife, Agatha, to marry a young courtesan. In contrast, Cleanthes and his wife, Hippolita, seek to save their father, Leonides, by hiding him and staging a funeral to suggest that he has died before reaching the age for execution. Instead of being sombre. the funeral is characterized by cheerful music, bright clothes and joyful behaviour, as Cleanthes and Hippolita rejoice that Leonides died a natural death.

There are three plots, serious, comic and farcical, each involving three main characters: Cleanthes, Hippolita and Leonides; Eugenia, Lysander and Simonides; Gnotho, Agatha and Siren. The first two are linked through kinship: Lysander is Cleanthes' uncle, and it is Cleanthes' condemnation of Eugenia's behaviour towards her husband that provokes her to reveal the secret of Leonides' concealment. The third plot is not linked directly with the others, as the roaring-school scenes are linked in *A Fair Quarrel*. This is surprising, and might be seen as a flaw in the play's structure. In an adaptation of *The Old Law* for the Commonweal Theatre Company's production at the Lyric Studio, Hammersmith, in 1990, Max Hafler made Gnotho Simonides' steward, thus tying the third plot more closely to the other two, very much in the spirit of Middleton and Rowley's usual practice.

*The Old Law* has been called 'one of the most extraordinary dramas in the Middleton canon'.[9] George E. Rowe Jr. skilfully identifies the subversive nature of the play. While Evander's law suggests at the beginning the triumph of youth over age that will renew society, a major theme of the New Comedy tradition, this is usually the conclusion of such plays. Here the law promotes a concern with death, and releases disintegrative forces that threaten social collapse if allowed to flourish. Comedy, as Rowe remarks, 'is transformed into nightmare'.[10] The characters who would have been the hero and heroine of a New Comedy, Simonides and Eugenia, are vicious and immoral, while the alternative hero and heroine, Cleanthes and Hippolita, though young, express the values and outlook of age, and are therefore unnatural or absurd in the world of the play. Rowe characterizes that world as one of 'irreconcilable conflicts and grotesque tensions',[11] which are not resolved by the ending. The 2005 Royal Shakespeare Company production by Sean Holmes was very successful in bringing out these features. The play was given its secondary title, *A New Way to Please You*, no doubt to make an unknown play sound more attractive. Critical commentaries have so far ignored this title, but its use by the

RSC suddenly reveals both an additional meaning in the primary title, and that the two titles need to be taken together: *The Old Law* has been understood as meaning either the law dealing with old people, or the Fifth Commandment, 'Honour thy father and thy mother', but, when juxtaposed to the second title, contrasts between old and new, past and present, are highlighted, providing a typically Middletonian shift of perspective. The first title may suggest that the action of the play takes place in the past; its extreme nature may provoke a complacent 'it-couldn't-happen-today' response in the audience: people are too civilized, enlightened and moral now. The second title, however, suggests the contrary: members of the same audience may well be pleased to find the play feeds fantasies of freedom and acquisition, making them wish that Evander's law applied to their own society. Though nominally set in Epire, the final scene of the RSC production, with a laddish Simonides and his cronies sitting in judgment, conveying an image of a dominant yob culture, and a legal system that rewarded the perpetrators of crimes while punishing the victims, clearly suggested contemporary Britain. This disturbing vision remained true to the original while connecting forcefully with the present.

The disturbing nature of *The Old Law* is reinforced by what in another tragicomedy might have been simply a highly contrived *deus ex machina* device to solve the problems Evander's law creates. For the first four acts the audience is allowed to view the Duke as a tyrant, an ally of self-seeking young men like Simonides. Only in the fifth act is it revealed that the law was a device by a morally upright prince to discover the true natures of his courtiers. It is a variation on the disguised-ruler convention used in *The Phoenix* and *Measure for Measure*. In *The Old Law* the audience suddenly has to change its assumptions about, and its view of, the ruler, but the dramatists do not allow a comfortable conclusion. Gnotho's appearance in the last scene raises questions about Evander's behaviour: not only whether he was right to risk confusing his subjects by changing laws, but also whether he was right, however good his intentions, to unleash the destructive forces of unrestrained self-seeking in his country, causing such unnecessary suffering to innocent people. The play's concerns mark it off from the other tragicomedies,

*The Witch, A Fair Quarrel* and *More Dissemblers Besides Women*, and its treatment of conflict between individual conscience and the law is a subject of enduring relevance. The other plays, with their concerns with seventeenth-century court scandal, duelling codes and religious matters, are more firmly rooted in their period.

*The Changeling* examines themes of constancy and change. Beatrice-Joanna is betrothed to Alonzo, chosen by her father, but falls in love with a stranger, Alsemero. So enamoured of him is she that she persuades De Flores, who is secretly infatuated with her, to kill Alonzo. This places her in his power, and, though she marries Alsemero, she is forced to become De Flores's mistress. The second plot, set in a madhouse, features two disguised courtiers who infiltrate in lustful pursuit of the keeper's wife, Isabella. The play provides a key site for discussion of dramatic collaboration. The process of 'disintegration' has tended to emphasize the separateness of the two plots. Yet this is at odds with another major concern of criticism: the remarkably unified and coherent nature of the play. Mooney, for instance, writes of its 'unique integral consistency'.[12] Nochimson considers how the implications of the unified nature of the play may develop our understanding of collaboration: 'we find a play marked by a thematic consistency that makes the concept of two playwrights working independently of each other on separate shares of the play seem highly improbable'.[13]

Like *A Fair Quarrel* and *The Old Law*, *The Changeling* has a clarity of narrative line and works on the principle of plots in contrasting modes, tragic and comic. The plots are linked not by kinship connections, but in a much more complex manner and on a number of levels. By setting one plot in a madhouse, the dramatists allow reflections on the actions of the supposedly sane in the other plot, which depicts metaphorical or moral madness. Reiteration of key words also binds the plots together,[14] and the term 'changeling', which has various meanings, may be applied to a number of characters in the play.[15] Episodes in one plot reflect those in the other: for instance, De Flores watches the meeting of Alsemero and Beatrice-Joanna, while Lollio similarly observes the meeting between Antonio and Isabella. Mooney notes that the structure is one of consecutive alternation of paired sets of scenes, which stress the interrelationship of the plots through parallel and contrast.[16]

The title suggests that a major concern will be with change, transference and metamorphosis, and, indeed, *The Changeling* not only alternates comic and tragic modes but also presents other contrasts and antitheses, though the elements of the play rarely consist of simple oppositions. Much critical energy has been expended on analysis of the powerfully intense Beatrice–De Flores scenes. One of their characteristics is the number of asides, which convey to the audience interior thoughts and desires set against exterior words and actions, and one of the most striking features throughout the play is its concern with secrets and concealment, interiority. This is linked with the spatial suggestiveness of the play as a whole, with contrasts involving the play's locations, between interior and exterior, light and darkness, and the ways physical space is used to emblematize mental and emotional space. These features might well have been enhanced by its original staging at an indoor theatre, The Phoenix. The 1988 National Theatre production brilliantly presented interior/exterior contrasts, with lighting in the opening scene that suggested the intense Spanish sun beating down, glimpsed later through latticed shutters in the interior scenes, making those interiors more shadowy by contrast. The first scene takes place outside the castle and close to the harbour, evoking the open air, sea and freedom of movement. At the end of the scene, when Alsemero has made his decision to stay, all the characters enter the castle, of which Vermandero says 'within are secrets' (*C.* I. i. 162). As the doors of the castle close, the action of the first plot moves from the freedom of the outside world to interior spaces, which become increasingly confined until, in the third act, De Flores leads the unwitting Alonzo through a maze of narrow passages, emphasized by the need to remove his sword, to his death in the deep recesses of the castle. The madhouse plot takes place entirely within confined interiors, while, in the last scene, Alsemero shuts Beatrice and De Flores in a closet, from which they emerge to deliver their death speeches. Beatrice envisages release in death in an image of blood taken from a sick person flowing out of the castle through the common sewer, echoing a similar image in *1 Honest Whore* (*HW* II. i. 324–6). To this state has she come from that hopeful and joyful entry into the fortress in the first act. Her motive in having Alonzo murdered by De Flores had been to gain the freedom to marry Alsemero, but with every turn she becomes increasingly restricted. The movement from exterior space to increasingly restricted interior spaces at the moment of the murder, and finally from interior to exterior space in the image of the blood flowing out of the castle at her death, emblematically suggests Beatrice's trajectory.

*The Changeling* also presents shifting perspectives and a radical instability of identity. Its main character has a double name, Beatrice-Joanna, which suggests contrasting characteristics: Beatrice signified an ideal of womanhood, while Joan was a common name given to a whore. However, ironically she is called Joanna through most of the play, as she pretends to be a paragon of virtue, and is referred to only once, at the end, as Beatrice, when her crimes have been revealed (C. V. iii. 148). Alsemero also provides a good example of a character who provokes different responses from the audience at various points in the play. He opens it with a speech informing us he has fallen in love with a woman he has seen in church. At this point spectators may well assume that this is the lover 'hero' of the play, with whom they are likely to be expected to empathize, and certainly if this were a comedy his spontaneous passion for Beatrice, which is opposed to her father's choice of husband, would normally generate audience approval. But this is not a comedy, and Alsemero's decision to stay in Alicante to pursue his desire leads Beatrice to commit murder to marry him. By Act IV the lover of the opening becomes transformed into the jealous husband of city comedy, afraid, like Alibius, of being cuckolded, as Beatrice creeps into his closet while he is out, and discovers that, far from being concerned with high and learned matters, her husband is sexually insecure, relying on virginity and pregnancy tests to test his wife's faithfulness. Yet by the last scene of the play Alsemero has regained stature and authority as he condemns Beatrice and De Flores to become the dominant voice at the close, including speaking the Epilogue.

De Flores, too, undergoes transformation. He begins a helpless victim of a love that is obsessive, unrequited and causes him great suffering, hated by Beatrice for his 'dog face' disfigurement. Having committed the murder, he changes, first to controlling villain as he gains power over her by knowing her secret, then to 'wondrous necessary man' (C. V. i. 90) as Beatrice comes to love him for his protection of that secret, and ends like a perverse version of the lover 'hero' of another kind of tragedy with a defiant assertion that he had gained Beatrice's love against the odds, that he had it totally, and that for him nothing else matters –

> DE FLORES. I lov'd this woman in spite of her heart;
> Her love I earn'd out of Piracquo's murder . . .
> . . . . .
>                         Yes, and her honour's prize
> Was my reward; I thank life for nothing
> But that pleasure; it was so sweet to me
> That I have drunk up all, left none behind
> For any man to pledge me.
>                                         (C. V. iii. 165–71)

De Flores bears some resemblance here to Vindice at the end of *The Revenger's Tragedy*, boasting about the wittiness of his revenge, and the image of drinking recalls Hengist's description of his ambition as a great thirst (*HKK* 2932–4).

Changes in audience perception of character are linked to the way *The Changeling*, like *The Old Law*, is constructed upon pairs and trios of characters. The pairing of Beatrice and Isabella in the two plots might seem at first to provide a simple contrast, and, indeed, has often been read as such, with Isabella an example of a woman who remains faithful to her vows: she is attracted by Antonio, but resists him, unlike Beatrice's response to Alsemero. However, a careful reading of Act IV, Scene iii suggests that the matter is more complex. In her disguise as a madwoman Isabella physically assaults Antonio in a very sexually suggestive manner.[17] Not recognizing her, he rejects her advances, and her response suggests she is disappointed that he is not a sufficiently clear-sighted lover to recognize her beneath her disguise, rating his love as shallow. She leaves with the words 'I came a feigner to return stark mad' (C. IV. iii. 123): she came pretending to be a disturbed person, but leaves truly emotionally disturbed. The line suggests that, had he responded differently, she would have acted differently, rather than that she has made a simple, virtuous decision. The pairing of Isabella and Beatrice is made still more complex by the presence of another female character, Diaphanta, who provides another kind of contrast to Beatrice, naive and pleasure-loving, as opposed to the calculating, vicious woman her mistress becomes.

Both central female characters are associated with trios of men who are in love with them: Beatrice with Alonzo, Alsemero and De Flores; Isabella with Antonio, Franciscus and Lollio. Within the trios there are pairings: in the early part of the play Alonzo with Alsemero, in the latter part Alsemero with De Flores. Antonio and Franciscus disguise themselves as the two different types within the madhouse, the fool and the madman. There are further pairings: Lollio is a comic reflection of De Flores, and Alibius of Vermandero, as the older authority figures in the two plots. But, as has been noted, momentarily in Act IV Alsemero becomes paired with Alibius, another example of the comic type of the jealous husband who is deceived by his wife.

This is then a play with very clear structural patterning, but also one in which the pattern does not remain static, undergoing constant kaleidoscopic rearrangement of its component parts so that an audience has to shift and reassess its responses to characters and issues. In this respect *The Changeling* perhaps provides insights into what the process of collaboration may have involved; indeed it may be seen as providing a suggestive conceit of the process itself.

The clear structure and unity the play displays could not have been achieved without the collaborators working closely together. At the same time, the constant shifting and rearrangement of the play's component parts may be regarded as reflecting the complex processes of negotiation, revision, reworking, deletion, reassessment and debate between the writers that must have been involved in the production of a work of such richness and depth. Moreover, the processes would have been ongoing, fluid and transformational; each stage could produce unforeseen effects and unexpected resonances, in turn suggesting new possibilities of development, some of which might have proved productive, others dead ends. If this in many respects describes the process of composition a solo writer would also go through, it serves to emphasize that, essentially, collaborative composition is little different. But the solo writer must make autonomous decisions about the different possibilities and potentialities of his material and ideas, and of their development, whereas a collaboration is the coming-together of two or more individuals who may have differing views, perspectives or ideas about the working-out of the play's themes, and differences of approach, expression and technique, which require reconciliation and resolution through debate, persuasion and interaction. On these matters John Jowett's examination of collaboration between Middleton and Shakespeare in *Timon of Athens* is illuminating.[18] It might be argued that the solo writer has the better chance of writing an aesthetically successful play because he has only himself to argue with; but, equally, tensions between contributors may generate the creative energy that produces a masterpiece. *The Changeling* is such a play, and above all demonstrates that the process of collaboration must have been as complex and subtle as the play it produced, indisputably their greatest success as a collaborative team.

# 6

# Intertextual Middleton

As we have seen, Middleton drew on and reworked textual motifs in the plays of other dramatists – *Hamlet* is a notable example. In this chapter we examine intertextuality in further detail. In view of the extensive number of illustrative examples and limited space we concentrate on two examples, one involving a play by John Marston and the other non-dramatic material by the poet Samuel Daniel. Both focus on female characters and debates about women, matters identified earlier as sources of considerable complexity and controversy in the work of Middleton and his collaborators.

We are here concerned not with how writers interact, but with how one text works with another. It may take the form of allusion, when even a single phrase may import a trace of another writer into the text.[1] It may also be a matter of genre, where other plays are invoked through use of conventions, or even by title, as in the case of *The Revenger's Tragedy*. As the chapter on Middleton and Shakespeare highlighted, we are dealing with performance texts, and it is important to remember that the medium is visual, so the dramatist may draw not only on words, but also on stage images. Similarly, a particular type of scene may evoke memories of other such scenes in other plays, as the wooing scene from *Richard III* may be recalled in the famous scene between Beatrice and De Flores in *The Changeling*.[2]

## *THE DUTCH COURTESAN* AND *THE CHANGELING*

John Marston's *The Dutch Courtesan* (1604) was originally a Queen's Revels play, as the title page of the 1605 edition indicates. This company combined with the Lady Elizabeth's

Men in March 1613, and performed *The Changeling* in 1622. Marston's play continued to be popular, being revived for the court by the Lady Elizabeth's Men on 25 February 1613, and repeated on 12 December the same year. It also appears, cancelled, on a list of plays, possibly being considered for court performance, on waste paper of the Revels' office, probably dating from 1619–20, so it may well have been in the repertory in 1622.

In a remarkable scene from *The Changeling* Beatrice manipulates De Flores by treating him with unwonted gentleness, even touching the face she finds repulsive, before indicating that she has something she desires him to do for her; he kneels down begging her to tell him what it is; and she finally reveals that she wishes him to murder Alonzo. This he gladly agrees to do, knowing it puts Beatrice in his power. In a later scene De Flores returns, having performed Beatrice's request, and as proof brings her Alonzo's ring. There are similarities here to a key scene in *The Dutch Courtesan*.[3] Malheureux, the melancholy man, is infatuated with Franceschina, the courtesan; she, however, loves Freevil, who ended their relationship on his marriage to another woman, also called Beatrice. Franceschina decides to use Malheureux, who has confessed his love to her, to murder Freevil. Like Beatrice in *The Changeling*, she uses physical contact: she kisses him and then tells him she is unable to respond to his protestations because she has sworn a vow. She keeps him on tenterhooks as he demands several times to know what it is, until finally she reveals it:

> MALHEUREUX. But what vow, what vow?
> FRANCESCHINA. So long as Freevil lives, I must not love.
> MALHEUREUX. Then he –
> FRANCESCHINA. Must –
> MALHEUREUX. Die.
> FRANCESCHINA. Ay. – No, there is no such vehemence in your affects. Would I were anything, so he were not!
>
> (*DC* II. ii. 173–9)

She then asks Malheureux to bring her Freevil's ring as proof that the deed has been performed. There are some details that differ, but the similarities are sufficiently close to suggest a resemblance for spectators. Martin Wiggins notes the plot similarities and the particular use of the lover as assassin, but there are also close resemblances in speech structure and stage images. In each scene there is a similar build-up of tension in the dialogue: the woman holds back from telling the man what she wants him to do, while he implores her to reveal it, and then there is a climactic release of tension in a series of broken lines as she finally tells him:

> BEATRICE. Then take him to thy fury!
> DE FLORES. I thirst for him.
> BEATRICE. Alonzo de Piracquo!
> DE FLORES. His end's upon him;
> He shall be seen no more.
>
> (C. II. ii. 133–5)

In a theatrical culture that depended on a wide repertory of plays owned and performed by a single company, it is probably safe to assume that regular playgoers at a particular theatre would be able to pick up echoes and cross references between the company's plays, and that writers, familiar with the company repertory, would use them knowing the audience might be able to draw such parallels. Martin Butler notes that many Caroline plays contained allusions to other plays and relied on the collaborative audience to pick them up,[4] and we may assume that a similar practice occurred in Jacobean plays. In some cases likenesses and connections may have resulted from the pressures of presenting a rapidly changing repertory, with little time to prepare a play for performance, making it necessary for the players to rely on stock acting conventions or ways of presenting particular kinds of scene. In other cases the earlier play may have carried a level of significance, possibly a political colouring, which then tinged the later play.

The resemblances between these two scenes are not solely in the verbal structures. In terms of movement and action, of stage pictures, there are also similarities: each woman makes physical contact with the man to persuade him to do what she wants, and if there were an acting tradition that Malheureux knelt to Franceschina, the connection might have been even clearer to an audience as the text indicates that De Flores kneels at this point: 'it's a service that I kneel for to you' (C. II. ii. 117). In Sam Walters's 1992 production of *The Dutch Courtesan* at the Orange Tree Theatre in Richmond-upon-Thames, Malheureux knelt, and this visual moment, together with the other details, made the similarity forcefully evident to members of the audience familiar with *The Changeling*.

Indeed, intertextual relations go further, extending to connections with Shakespeare. The scene from *The Dutch Courtesan* has been recognized as a reworking of the climactic 'Kill Claudio' episode from *Much Ado About Nothing* (1598),[5] a play Middleton quotes elsewhere in several places. It may be mere coincidence that all three plays contain characters named Beatrice – the name had been an obvious one since Dante to suggest an ideal of womanhood – but the intertextual connection here is apparent. It is impossible to tell whether Middleton and Rowley simply saw in the scene in *The Dutch Courtesan* the germ of a good dramatic idea that could be developed more effectively, or whether Marston's play had a level of contemporary significance lost to us, which might have been a reason for invoking it in 1622.

Another conjunction between *Much Ado About Nothing* and *The Dutch Courtesan* might suggest the latter to be the case: they were both selected for court performance during the celebrations for the wedding of James I's daughter, Princess Elizabeth, to the Protestant champion Elector Frederick, in 1613. This in itself might again have been coincidence, but when they are considered in connection with some of the other plays chosen for court performance at that time another possibility arises. *Othello* (1604) and *The Winter's Tale* (1609–11), dealing with marital jealousy and murder, might seem strange choices for entertainments at a marriage, but, like *Much Ado About Nothing*, they feature a pure woman who is traduced and declared a whore, a pattern that recurs in writings about the conflict between Protestantism and Catholicism. If these plays chosen for performance provided symbolic religio-political narratives appropriate to Princess Elizabeth's marriage, *The Dutch Courtesan*, with its figures of the whore (Franceschina) and the pure woman (Beatrice), might also have carried levels of reference no longer accessible to us. This must all remain a matter of conjecture, but it is possible that Middleton and Rowley's reworking of Marston's scene was not simply a convenient development of material in the company's repertory, but also a means of signalling the play's religious and political orientation.

## DANIEL, SHAKESPEARE, MIDDLETON AND ROWLEY

Texts acquire histories and accretions of significance through use and reuse in particular contexts and through various modes of presentation. When a writer consciously invokes a text, he calls up a context and a history of reading. The pamphlets on which Middleton drew in *A Game at Chess* all had political colouring as Protestant propaganda. So too, when Middleton and Rowley took a story from John Reynolds's *The Triumphs of God's Revenge* (1621) for the main plot of *The Changeling*, they chose a source that bewailed the iniquities of contemporary society and carried covert references to the Overbury murder scandal. In this case it is just possible that some members of an audience would have read Reynolds and been aware how this particular story had been used, even though the dramatists do not invoke Reynolds directly. However, more direct and widespread audience recognition of textual collaboration is likely to occur when the dramatist uses a narrative that has acquired some symbolic meaning through use in earlier texts. Invocation of those texts may be evident from the mere use of a particular kind of narrative, such as myth. One such instance is the story of Lucrece, which, together with the motif of the chaste ideal threatened, contaminated and destroyed, recurs in Middleton works from the early days of his writing career when he produced his poem, *The Ghost of Lucrece* (1600). It is found in the two Castizas of *The Revenger's Tragedy* and *Hengist, King of Kent*, the Lady in *The Lady's Tragedy*, the Duchess in *More Dissemblers Besides Women*, and finds rather more complex and indirect reference in *Women Beware Women*, *The Changeling*, and *A Game at Chess*, in which rapes occur or are attempted. The immediate connection Middleton's *Lucrece* suggests is with Shakespeare's poem *The Rape of Lucrece* (1594), especially as Middleton uses the same rime royal stanza and borrows freely from it. However, it is necessary to look back beyond Shakespeare's poem to a text that had considerably influenced it in turn, Samuel Daniel's *The Complaint of Rosamond* (1592). It was also written in rime royal and influenced many poets in the decade or so after its publication. Printed in the 1592 authorized edition of Daniel's sonnet sequence *To Delia*, it formed a companion piece to the sequence, setting up a dialectical opposition. *The Complaint of*

*Rosamond* tells the story not of an imagined ideal, as Delia may be, but of a historical personage, Rosamond Clifford, who became mistress to Henry II and was murdered by his queen. It begins, as often in the complaint tradition to which it belongs, with the appearance of her ghost, just as the spirit of Lucrece rises at the beginning of Middleton's poem. She implores the poet-lover of Delia to tell her story to the world so that she can gain rest in the underworld. Rosamond becomes the narrator of her personal history, and thus in *The Complaint of Rosamond* we hear the woman's voice and ostensibly see events from a female perspective, in contrast to the sonnet sequence, in which the woman remains silent and the male lover's perspective is projected. The Petrarchan idealism of the sonnet sequence is set against the realism of the complaint. The poet-lover begs Delia to imparadise him, while Rosamond tells how she is 'unparadised'. In the sonnet sequence Delia remains chaste to the end and stays in the country, whereas Rosamond Clifford comes from the country to the court, where her vanity is encouraged by the courtly love conventions that elevate her to a position of power, so that even the king becomes her servant.

The poet-lover of the sonnet sequence attempts to persuade Delia to respond to him by use of the *carpe diem* argument. This is the very argument used by an older, experienced female courtier to persuade Rosamond to give herself to the king. The complaint encourages the reader to reflect back upon the sonnet sequence, and to reread it from a different perspective. The dialectical arrangement of sonnets and complaint problematizes the integrity of the Petrarchan lover in the sonnets, and lays less stress on the culpability of the woman in the complaint, thus providing a critique of courtly attitudes and values.

There are strong suggestions of intertextual links between both *Women Beware Women* and *The Changeling,* and Daniel's poem. In *Women Beware Women* the motif of the young girl desired by the ruler and corrupted by a court lady, Livia, is central. Indeed, echoes of Rosamond's confession may be detected in Livia's comments on habituation to sin:

My flesh gan loathe the new-felt touch of sinning.
Shame leaves us by degrees, not at first winning:
For Nature checks a new offence with loathing:

But use of sin doth make it seem as nothing.

(*CR*, ll. 499-62)

LIVIA. 'Tis but a qualm of honour, 'twill away;
A little bitter for the time, but lasts not.
Sin tastes at the first draught like wormwood water,
But, drunk again, 'tis nectar ever after.

(*WBW* II. ii. 476-9)

Just as Guardiano prepares Bianca for her unexpected encounter with the Duke by showing her the 'naked pictures' in Livia's gallery, so the King sends Rosamond a casket on which are engraved figures from mythological narratives involving encounters of gods with nymphs and women. The significance of the choice of this particular gift is not made clear: Rosamond reads the artwork as providing potential warnings to her, which she ignores, but this would hardly have been the King's intention. In the description of Amymone's struggles with Neptune on the casket, her struggles and tears are shown as simply increasing his passion, a detail present in Shakepeare's *The Rape of Lucrece* and also in the scene of Bianca's rape.

There are also a number of resemblances between the Middleton scene and the Shakespeare poem. There is the common gestural feature of the hand on the breast: 'I feel thy breast shake like a turtle panting│Under a loving hand that makes much on't' (*WBW* II. ii. 323-4); 'His hand that yet remains upon her breast – │ Rude ram, to batter such an ivory wall' (*RL*, ll. 463-4). Although Shakespeare uses the image of the woman as a beseiged city or fortress, common in Petrarchan love poetry, he has already in the previous stanza associated her with a bird that 'trembling lies' (*RL*, ll. 457). In both play and poem the ravisher praises the victim's beauty, but warns that his passion is so strong he is prepared to use force if she does not yield: struggling only serves to increase his lust.

As we have seen, the fortress is a central image in *The Changeling*: Vermandero's castle in which he keeps his daughter, and Beatrice-Joanna imaged as a castle penetrated by the enemy, a violation of the Petrarchan ideal of the virtuous woman laid siege to by the unrequited lover.[6] Shakespeare's *The Rape of Lucrece* uses similar imagery: not only is Tarquin's hand described as a battering ram, but later Lucrece looks at pictures of the siege and entry of Troy and finds parallels to her own situation. *The Changeling* looks critically at Petrarchan attitudes, and, as critics have noted,[7] draws upon another central Petrarchan conceit, the maze or labyrinth, as do Daniel's sonnet sequence and *The Complaint of Rosamond*. In the sonnets it is the lover who is lost in the maze, but in *The Complaint of Rosamond* Rosamond herself is hidden by Henry II in a stately palace full of intricate passages. Beatrice, realizing with panic that she is out of her depth in dealing with the demanding De Flores, cries: 'I'm in a labyrinth' (*C*. III. iv. 71), while Isabella, disguised as a madwoman, cries out to Antonio: 'Stand up, thou son of Cretan Dedalus|And let us tread the lower labyrinth' (*C*. IV. iii. 94–6). Vermandero's fortress is full of narrow and intricate passages, a maze to which De Flores has the keys, a place of horror where Alonso is murdered and Beatrice loses her way. The castle in *The Complaint of Rosamond* is likened to the Cretan labyrinth, Rosamond describing herself as 'the Minotaure of shame' (*CR*, l. 485). She perceives herself transformed into a monster, a changeling, by sin. In the last scenes great emphasis is placed upon Beatrice's transformation and her monstrousness: 'O, thou art all deformed!' (*C*. V. iii. 77), Alsemero cries.

Yet, despite these intertextual connections, *The Changeling* is a profoundly different text from Daniel's. Daniel uses the story of Rosamond to present a confessional release; Middleton and Rowley present a portrait of irrevocable damnation. Daniel's dialectical arrangement of sonnets and complaint presents a critical view of the Petrarchan lover, and Rosamond's downfall is as much the result of male courtly attitudes to women as her own weakness. Middleton and Rowley's critical focus on Petrarchism reinforces the harshness of the ridicule and condemnation of Beatrice, who has pretended to be the virtuous Petrarchan beloved. However, *Women Beware Women* differs somewhat in this respect. As was suggested in Chapter 1, it may be read as an indictment of patriarchal attitudes, which by idealizing women corrupt them with a sense of power, and in this respect it is closer to *The Complaint of Rosamond*.

The Lucrece story was a topos for the expression of conflicts between body and spirit, between different aspects of human nature, and between licence and control; but it also provided a site for discussion of both political and gender issues. Zara

Bruzzi is struck by the many echoes in Daniel's sonnet sequence of Protestant religious discourse, and detects 'a subtle modulation of Petrarchan discourse into Protestant discourse' whereby Delia becomes 'a pattern of Protestant womanhood'.[8] The invocation of Daniel's *To Delia* and *The Complaint of Rosamond* in *Women Beware Women* and *The Changeling* places the tragedies in the context of religious and political debates. Middleton was not alone in the 1620s in invoking *The Complaint of Rosamond* from the 1590s: Patrick Hannay's poem *Sheretine and Mariana* (1622), a text that deals covertly with political matters and especially with the plight of James's daughter, Elizabeth, and her husband, the Elector Frederick, derives from it.[9] By the 1620s the Overbury murder, the figure of Frances Howard, worries about Catholic subversion and the way in which court women might be used for this purpose gave these debates a sharp contemporary slant. The kinds of intertextual collaboration examined here placed current scandals in a wider context, revealed their connection with questions that early modern society had long been debating, and highlighted their implications for the future.

## MIDDLETON AND MIDDLETON

Middleton's persistent return to the Lucrece motif draws attention to a final kind of collaboration, his collaboration not only with the work of others but with his own texts. The self-referential quality of Middleton texts has often been noted. Situations, characters and images, for instance, are reworked by the writer in different generic contexts. As R. H. Barker notes, Vindice in *The Revenger's Tragedy* and Follywit in *A Mad World, My Masters* are related as clever men who become blinded by their own cleverness, the one in a tragedy, the other in a comedy. In *Hengist, King of Kent* Middleton reworks the situation of the players who perform a play as a cover for robbing their host in *A Mad World, My Masters*. Another obvious example is chess, which features centrally in *Women Beware Women* and *A Game at Chess*. Repetition invites rereadings. Thus the fact that the motif of the chess game is used for a political satire might make us ask questions about whether there was a political dimension to the earlier use of the image in *Women Beware Women*. A very important scene in *Hengist, King of Kent* shows the murderous deception of the Saxons, who hide their battleaxes, intending to use them later to slaughter the Britons at a supposedly peaceful meeting on Salisbury Plain. In *The Changeling* there is an unusual stage direction between Acts II and III: *'In the act-time De Flores hides a naked rapier.'* This is a rare, if not unique, stage direction for the hiding of a property in plays of the period,[10] and an unusual instance of an action between the acts (when the candles would have been changed), which is clearly not a 'stage-management' instruction for the placing of a property but an indication of what the audience is intended to see as part of the action. This moment recalls the Saxons in *Hengist, King of Kent*, where the historical material is used to draw a parallel with threats of Catholic infiltration and subversion. The most recent editor of the play refers to it as 'one of the most popular and performed plays of the 1620s and 1630s';[11] if so, it is reasonable to assume that there were likely to be spectators who had seen both plays. They would, therefore, have been able to make connections and ask questions about political suggestiveness in the character of De Flores.

We cannot know what was in the writer's mind, and the danger is that there is a tendency for readers to fix on such apparent connections to form a seamless, unified and comprehensive view of a writer's work. The work of Middleton, both alone and with his collaborators, resists such attempts, not least on the matter of gender issues. The texts as a whole do have some continuities, but they also provide evidence, through shifting perspectives, not of settled and fixed views but of continuing and continuous discussion of key contemporary issues. The strands change, or are arranged differently, and their appearance in a new context changes the weave. Self-reference in the current work then becomes reference to past positions, which are then re-examined. The desire to find the unitary author founders in the face of multiple Middletons.

# Afterword

> Quests for my own words are quests for a word that is not my own.
>
> <div align="right">(Mikhail Bakhtin, <i>Speech Genres and Other Late Essays</i>, 1986)</div>

'Collaboration', rather than 'authorship', is an appropriate term to describe not only early modern playwriting but the process by which the playhouse brought plays to life. Col*labor*ation – the labour that lies within the process[1] – writ large signifies the work done by numerous hands, many unknown, in bringing the play to a tangible form. Thus writers, patrons, actors, printers, compositors in turn all bring into play earlier texts and remembered theatrical moments, which served as sources on which playwrights drew, and later writers and editors have continued to draw, right up to the present. Howard Barker's version of *Women Beware Women* (1986) and Alex Cox's film *Revengers Tragedy* (2002), like Middleton's adaptation of *Measure for Measure* (1621), are instances of posthumous collaboration, where the original 'author' has been bypassed: what Middleton does with 'Shakespeare', modern collaborators do with 'Middleton'. But the mediation process by which an early modern play is edited, printed and categorized also brings the scholar and editor into a collaborative relationship with the text. This is nowhere more evident than in the case of Middleton. He was long regarded as an important dramatist ranking just below Jonson and Marlowe; now his critical fortunes are tied closely to the canon, and equally importantly with his connection with Shakespeare. This is unfortunate but inevitable. The Oxford Middleton may do for Middleton what the First Folio did for Shakespeare, but in neither case can any of the texts be placed outside a collaborative matrix, spanning both the past and the immediate present.

Writing about Middleton entails writing about collaboration; but it also raises the issues of canon and attribution. This book declared at the outset that determining playwrights' 'shares' in a given text is not its primary concern: for reasons of space, too, collaboration, rather than disintegration, is its focus. Yet clearly the canon is bound up with attribution issues, and since the 1950s Middleton studies have been dominated by this question. It remains here to return, briefly, to this matter, and suggest ways in which an approach that focuses on collaboration may lead to deeper insights into the text.

As John Jowett has recently proposed, where a scholarly consensus on the division of a text between two or more authors exists, this 'can constructively lead into a critical, interpretative practice'.[2] That is, a text can be regarded as a dialogue, not between two or more playwrights as such but between the textual presences in the play. Such an approach, recalling Mikhail Bakhtin's theory of 'polyphony', or competing voices, reminds us that a text is made up of myriad components. While attribution studies are bound up with the question of authorship, and recent notions such as accommodation theory imply a compositional consensus that results in a textual 'whole', the idea of a dialogue is something of a halfway house. But perhaps most significantly it may lead to a wider recognition that the text is a multiply-constituted palimpsest. Thus we might move away from 'authorship', and the illusion of a *synchronic* text, to the collaboration of voices that is the *diachronic* text, a 'presenting' of earlier texts to which additions may be made, and remade, in the 're-presenting' of the early modern theatre of Middleton and his collaborators.

# Notes

**PREFACE**

1. Roland Barthes, 'From Work to Text' (1971), in *Image – Music –Text*, ed. and trans. Stephen Heath (London: Fontana, 1977), 159.

**INTRODUCTION**

1. Thomas Dekker, *The Gull's Hornbook*, ed. R. B. McKerrow (London: De La More Press, 1904), 49.
2. G. E. Bentley, *The Profession of Dramatist in Shakespeare's Time, 1590–1642* (Princeton: Princeton University Press, 1971), 199.
3. Gary Taylor, 'Forms of Opposition: Shakespeare and Middleton', *English Literary Renaissance*, 24 (1994), 283–314.
4. T. S. Eliot, 'Thomas Middleton', in *Elizabethan Dramatists* (London: Faber, 1963), 84.
5. Margot Heinemann, *Puritanism and Theatre: Thomas Middleton and Opposition Drama under the Early Stuarts* (Cambridge: Cambridge University Press, 1980); Jerzy Limon, *Dangerous Matter: English Drama and Politics 1623/24* (Cambridge: Cambridge University Press, 1986); A. A. Bromham and Zara Bruzzi, *'The Changeling' and the Years of Crisis 1619–1624: A Hieroglyph of Britain* (London: Pinter, 1990); Martin White, *Middleton and Tourneur* (Basingstoke: Macmillan, 1992).
6. Eliot, 'Thomas Middleton', 83.
7. Ibid. 88.
8. Jeffrey A. Masten, 'Playwrighting: Authorship and Collaboration', in John D. Cox and David Scott Kastan (eds.), *A New History of Early English Drama* (New York: Columbia University Press, 1997), 358.
9. Brian Gibbons, *Jacobean City Comedy: A Study of Satiric Plays by Jonson, Marston and Middleton*, 2nd edn. (London: Methuen, 1980).
10. Leo Salingar, 'Jacobean Playwrights and "Judicious" Spectators', *Renaissance Drama*, 22 (1991), 209–34.

# CHAPTER 1

1. Richard Dutton, 'Introduction', in Thomas Middleton, *'Women Beware Women' and Other Plays*, ed. Dutton (Oxford: Oxford University Press, 1999), p. xv.
2. A. L. Beier and Roger Finlay, *London 1500–1700: The Making of the Metropolis* (London: Longman, 1986), 51.
3. Gary Taylor and John Jowett, *Shakespeare Reshaped 1606–1623* (Oxford: Clarendon Press, 1993), 107–236.
4. Michael Taylor, 'Introduction', in Thomas Middleton, *'A Mad World, My Masters' and Other Plays*, ed. Michael Taylor (Oxford: Oxford University Press, 1995), p. xi.
5. Michael Hattaway, 'Drama and Society', in A. R. Braunmuller and Michael Hattaway (eds.), *The Cambridge Companion to Renaissance Drama* (Cambridge: Cambridge University Press, 2003), 108.
6. William R. Dynes, 'The Trickster Figure in Jacobean City Comedy', *Studies in English Literature*, 33 (1993), 367.
7. James Knowles, 'The Spectacle of the Realm: Civic Consciousness, Rhetoric and Ritual in Early Modern London', in J. R. Mulryne and Margaret Shewring (eds.), *Theatre and Government under the Early Stuarts* (Cambridge: Cambridge University Press, 1993), 180.
8. Robert Brenner, *Merchants and Revolution: Commercial Change, Political Conflict, and London's Overseas Traders, 1550–1653* (Princeton: Princeton University Press, 1993), 199–201.
9. A. A. Bromham, 'Thomas Middleton's *The Triumphs of Truth*: City Politics in 1613', *The Seventeenth Century*, 10 (1995), 1–25.
10. John Twyning, *London Dispossessed: Literature and Social Space in the Early Modern City* (Basingstoke: Macmillan, 1998), 64.
11. Alastair Bellany, *The Politics of Court Scandal in Early Modern England: News Culture and the Overbury Affair, 1603–1660* (Cambridge: Cambridge University Press, 2002), 181–211.
12. Ibid. 136-180.
13. Thomas Middleton, *The Second Maiden's Tragedy*, ed. Anne Lancashire (Manchester: Manchester University Press, 1978), App. A, pp. 278–89; Grace Ioppolo, 'Sexual Treason, Treasonous Sexuality, and the Eventful Politics of James I in Middleton's *Hengist, King of Kent*', *Ben Jonson Journal*, 3 (1996), 97–103.
14. Anne Lancashire, 'Introduction', in Middleton, *The Second Maiden's Tragedy*, ed. Lancashire, 38–49.
15. Ibid. 44.
16. A. A. Bromham and Zara Bruzzi,*'The Changeling' and the Years of Crisis 1619–1624: A Hieroglyph of Britain* (London: Pinter, 1990), 156–65.

17. Elizabeth Schafer 'Introduction', in Thomas Middleton, *The Witch*, ed. Elizabeth Schafer (London: A. & C. Black, 1994), p. xvi.
18. Nicholas Brooke, *Horrid Laughter in Jacobean Tragedy* (London: Open Books, 1979).
19. Zara Bruzzi, 'A Device to Fit the Times: Intertextual Allusion in Thomas Middleton's *Women Beware Women*', in Michele Marrapodi and A. J. Hoenselaars (eds.), *The Italian World of English Renaissance Drama: Cultural Exchange and Intertextuality* (Newark, Del.: University of Delaware Press, 1998), 302–20.
20. Margot Heinemann, *Puritanism and Theatre: Thomas Middleton and Opposition Drama under the Early Stuarts* (Cambridge: Cambridge University Press, 1980); John Stachniewski, 'Calvinist Psychology in Middleton's Tragedies', in R. V. Holdsworth (ed.), *Three Jacobean Revenge Tragedies* (Basingstoke: Macmillan, 1990), 226–46.
21. Irving Ribner, *Jacobean Tragedy: The Quest for Moral Order* (London: Methuen, 1962; repr. 1979), 138.
22. Richard Dutton, *Mastering the Revels: The Regulation and Censorship of English Renaissance Drama* (Iowa City: University of Iowa Press, 1991), 194–204; Janet Clare, *'Art made tongue-tied by authority': Elizabethan and Jacobean Dramatic Censorship*, 2nd edn. (Manchester: Manchester University Press, 1999), 179–86.
23. Bromham and Bruzzi, *'The Changeling' and the Years of Crisis 1619–1624*, 166–9.

## CHAPTER 2

1. Michel Foucault, 'What is an Author?' (1984), in Paul Rabinow (ed.), *The Foucault Reader: An Introduction to Foucault's Thought*, trans. Josue V. Harari (London: Penguin, 1991), 118.
2. Ibid. 105.
3. Grace Ioppolo, 'The Transmission of an English Renaissance Play-Text', in Arthur F. Kinney (ed.), *A Companion to Renaissance Drama* (Oxford: Blackwell, 2002), 170.
4. Jeffrey A. Masten, *Textual Intercourse: Collaboration, Authorship, and Sexualities in Renaissance Drama* (Cambridge: Cambridge University Press, 1997).
5. Ibid.
6. G. E. Bentley, *The Profession of Dramatist in Shakespeare's Time, 1590–1642* (Princeton: Princeton University Press, 1971), 199.
7. Jeffrey A. Masten, 'Playwrighting: Authorship and Collaboration', in John D. Cox and David Scott Kastan (eds.), *A New History of Early English Drama* (New York: Columbia University Press, 1997), 375–6.
8. Bentley, *The Profession of Dramatist*, 198; emphasis added.

9. Stephen Orgel, 'What is a Text?' (1981), in David Scott Kastan and Peter Stallybrass (eds.), *Staging the Renaissance: Reinterpretations of Elizabethan and Jacobean Drama* (London: Routledge, 1991), 84.
10. Ibid.; emphasis original.
11. Bentley, *The Profession of Dramatist*.
12. Orgel, 'What is a Text?', 86.
13. J. S. Cunningham, ed., *Tamburlaine* (Manchester: Manchester University Press, 1981), p. 111.
14. D. J. Lake, *The Canon of Thomas Middleton's Plays* (Cambridge: Cambridge University Press, 1975); MacDonald P. Jackson, *Studies in Attribution: Middleton and Shakespeare* (Salzburg Studies in English Literature: Jacobean Drama Studies 39; Salzburg; Institut für Sprache und Literatur, Universität Salzburg, 1979); Jonathan Hope, *The Authorship of Shakespeare's Plays: A Socio-Linguistic Study* (Cambridge: Cambridge University Press, 1994).
15. R. J. Street and H. Giles, 'Speech Accommodation Theory: A Social and Cognitive Approach to Language and Speech Behaviour', in Michael E. Roloff and Charles R. Berger (eds.), *Social Cognition and Communication* (Beverly Hills, Calif.: Sage Publications, 1982); Hope, *The Authorship of Shakespeare's Plays*, 79.
16. Stephen Greenblatt, *Shakespearean Negotiations: The Circulation of Social Energy* (Oxford: Clarendon Press, 1988), 1.
17. *The Norton Shakespeare. Based on the Oxford Edition*, ed. Stephen Greenblatt et al. (New York: W. W. Norton & Company, 1997), 3349.
18. T. S. Eliot, 'Thomas Middleton', in *Elizabethan Dramatists* (London: Faber, 1963), 84.
19. Margot Heinemann, *Puritanism and Theatre: Thomas Middleton and Opposition Drama under the Early Stuarts* (Cambridge: Cambridge University Press, 1980); John Jowett, 'Thomas Middleton', in Arthur F. Kinney (ed.), *A Companion to Renaissance Drama* (Oxford: Blackwell, 2002), 507–23.
20. *Henslowe's Diary*, ed. R. A. Foakes, 2nd edn. (Cambridge: Cambridge University Press, 2002), 201 (spelling slightly modernized).
21. Sara Jane Steen, *Ambrosia in an Earthern Vessel: Three Centuries of Audience and Reader Response to the Works of Thomas Middleton* (New York: AMS Press, 1993), 35.
22. Eliot, 'Thomas Middleton', 83.
23. G. E. Bentley, *The Jacobean and Caroline Stage* (7 vols.; Oxford: Clarendon Press, 1941–68), iv. 555.

## CHAPTER 3

1. Andrew Gurr, 'The Authority of the Globe and the Fortune', in

Lena Cowen Orlin (ed.), *Material London, Ca. 1600* (Philadelphia: University of Pennsylvania Press, 2000), 252.
2. G. E. Bentley, *The Profession of Dramatist in Shakespeare's Time, 1590–1642* (Princeton: Princeton University Press, 1971), 28.
3. *Henslowe's Diary*, ed. R. A. Foakes, 2nd edn. (Cambridge: Cambridge University Press, 2002), 209.
4. Julia Gasper, *The Dragon and the Dove: The Plays of Thomas Dekker* (Oxford: Clarendon Press, 1990), 62.
5. Kathleen E. McLuskie, *Dekker and Heywood* (Basingstoke: Macmillan, 1994), 25.
6. Elizabeth Cook, 'Introduction', in *The Roaring Girl*, ed. Elizabeth Cook (London: A. & C. Black, 1997), p. xvi.
7. Steven Mullaney, *The Place of the Stage: License, Play, and Power in Renaissance England* (Chicago: University of Chicago Press, 1988).
8. Andrew Gurr, *The Shakespeare Company, 1594–1642* (Cambridge: Cambridge University Press, 2004), 261; Mark Hutchings, 'Anti-Theatrical Prejudice and *1 Honest Whore*', *Notes and Queries*, 250 (2005), 220–1.
9. Viviana Comensoli, 'Merchants and Madcaps: Dekker's *Honest Whore* Plays and the *Commedia dell'arte*', in Michele Marrapodi *et al.* (eds.), *Shakespeare's Italy: Functions of Italian Locations in Renaissance Drama* (Manchester: Manchester University Press, 1993), 125–39.
10. McLuskie, *Dekker and Heywood*, 72–4.
11. John Twyning, *London Dispossessed: Literature and Social Space in the Early Modern City* (Basingstoke: Macmillan, 1998), 11.
12. Ibid.
13. Stephen Orgel, *Impersonations: The Performance of Gender in Shakespeare's England* (Cambridge: Cambridge University Press, 1996), 98.
14. Quoted in Jean E. Howard, 'Crossdressing, the Theatre, and Gender Struggle in Early Modern England', *Shakespeare Quarterly*, 39 (1988), 422.
15. Lisa Jardine, *Still Harping on Daughters: Women and Drama in the Age of Shakespeare* (Brighton: Harvester Press, 1983), 155.
16. D. J. Lake, *The Canon of Thomas Middleton's Plays* (Cambridge: Cambridge University Press, 1975), 63.
17. Ibid.; MacDonald P. Jackson, *Studies in Attribution: Middleton and Shakespeare* (Salzburg Studies in English Literature: Jacobean Drama Studies 39; Salzburg: Institut für Sprache und Literatur, Universität Salzburg, 1979).
18. Paul Mulholland, 'Introduction', in Thomas Middleton, *The Roaring Girl*, ed. Mulholland (Manchester: Manchester University Press, 1987), 8.
19. Paul Mulholland, 'The Date of *The Roaring Girl*', *Review of English Studies*, 28 (1977), 18.

20. Mulholland, 'Introduction', 9.
21. Ibid. 13.
22. Quoted in Middleton, *The Roaring Girl*, ed. Mulholland, App. E, p. 262.
23. Orgel, *Impersonations*, 107.
24. Quoted in Middleton, *The Roaring Girl*, ed. Mulholland, App. E, pp. 262–3.
25. Jean E. Howard, 'Crossdressing, the Theatre, and Gender Struggle in Early Modern England', *Shakespeare Quarterly*, 39 (1988), 418–40; David Cressy, 'Gender Trouble and Cross-Dressing in Early Modern England', *Journal of British Studies*, 35 (1996), 438–65.
26. Mulholland, 'Introduction', 14.
27. Lisa Jardine, *Still Harping on Daughters: Women and Drama in the Age of Shakespeare* (Brighton: Harvester Press, 1983), 160; Stephen Orgel, 'The Subtexts of *The Roaring Girl*', in Susan Zimmerman (ed.), *Erotic Politics: Desire on the Renaissance Stage* (London: Routledge, 1992), 23.
28. Orgel, 'The Subtexts of *The Roaring Girl*', 13; Jean E. Howard, 'Sex and Social Conflict: The Erotics of *The Roaring Girl*', in Susan Zimmerman, (ed.), *Erotic Politics: Desire on the Renaissance Stage* (London: Routledge, 1992), 176.
29. Marjorie Garber, 'The Logic of the Transvestite', in David Scott Kastan and Peter Stallybrass (eds.), *Staging the Renaissance: Reinterpretations of Elizabethan and Jacobean Drama* (London: Routledge, 1991), 225.
30. Howard, 'Sex and Social Conflict', 184.
31. Peter Stallybrass, 'Worn Worlds: Clothes and Identity on the Renaissance Stage', in Margreta de Grazia *et al.* (eds.), *Subject and Object in Renaissance Culture* (Cambridge: Cambridge University Press, 1996), 289.
32. Jardine, *Still Harping on Daughters*, 45.
33. Andrew Gurr, *The Shakespearean Stage 1574–1642*, 3rd edn. (Cambridge: Cambridge University Press, 1992), 83.
34. Stallybrass, 'Worn Worlds', 310.
35. See title page reproduced in Middleton, *The Roaring Girl*, ed. Mulholland, 71.
36. Mary Beth Rose, 'Women in Men's Clothes: Apparel and Social Stability in *The Roaring Girl*', *English Literary Renaissance*, 14 (1984), 367–91; repr. in Arthur F. Kinney and Dan S. Collins (eds), *Renaissance Historicism: Selections from 'English Literary Renaissance'* (Amherst, Mass.: University of Massachusetts Press, 1987), 223–47, at 242.
37. *Plays on Women*, eds. Kathleen McLuskie and David Bevington (Manchester: Manchester University Press, 1999), 178 n.
38. Walter Benjamin, 'Paris, Capital of the Nineteenth Century', in

Peter Demetz (ed.), *Reflections: Essays, Aphorisms, Autobiographical Writings*, trans. Edmund Jephcott (New York: Schocken Books, 1978), 146–62.
39. Janette Dillon, 'Fashion, Nation and Theatre in Late Sixteenth-Century London', in Edward J. Esche (ed.), *Shakespeare and his Contemporaries in Performance* (London: Ashgate, 2000), 165.
40. Ibid. 167.
41. Quoted in Middleton, *The Roaring Girl*, ed. Mulholland, App. E, p. 262.
42. Mulholland, 'The Date of *The Roaring Girl*', 22; Cook, 'Introduction', p. xviii.
43. Orgel, *Impersonations*, 8, 145–6.
44. Levin, Richard, 'Women in the Renaissance Theatre Audience', *Shakespeare Quarterly*, 40 (1989), 171.
45. Garber, 'The Logic of the Transvestite', 221.

## CHAPTER 4

1. Jeffrey A. Masten, *Textual Intercourse: Collaboration, Authorship, and Sexualities in Renaissance Drama* (Cambridge: Cambridge University Press, 1997).
2. Eric Rasmussen, 'Shakespeare's Hand in *"The Second Maiden's Tragedy"*', *Shakespeare Quarterly*, 40 (1989), 1–26; 'Reply to MacD. P. Jackson', *Shakespeare Quarterly*, 41 (1990), 406–7.
3. Brian Vickers, *Shakespeare, Co-Author: A Historical Study of Five Collaborative Plays* (Oxford: Oxford University Press, 2002), 244, 257, 264.
4. William, Shakespeare, *The Complete Works*, ed. Stanley Wells *et al.* (Oxford: Clarendon Press, 1986); *Timon of Athens*, ed. John Jowett (London: Thomas Nelson & Sons, 2004).
5. Nicholas Brooke, 'Introduction' in William Shakespeare, *Macbeth*, ed. Brooke (Oxford: Oxford University Press, 1990), 57.
6. *The Complete Works*, ed. Wells *et al.*; *Macbeth*, ed. Brooke.
7. *The Complete Works*, ed. Wells *et al.*; Gary Taylor and John Jowett, *Shakespeare Reshaped 1606–1623* (Oxford: Clarendon Press, 1993), 107–236.
8. D. J. Lake, *The Canon of Thomas Middleton's Plays* (Cambridge: Cambridge University Press, 1975).
9. MacDonald P. Jackson, *Studies in Attribution: Middleton and Shakespeare* (Salzburg Studies in English Literature: Jacobean Drama Studies 39; Salzburg: Institut für Sprache und Literatur, Universität Salzburg, 1979).
10. Rasmussen, 'Shakespeare's Hand'; 'Reply to MacD. P. Jackson'.

11. MacDonald P. Jackson, 'The Additions to *"The Second Maiden's Tragedy"*: Shakespeare or Middleton?', *Shakespeare Quarterly*, 41 (1990), 402–5.
12. Elizabeth Schafer, 'Introduction', in Thomas Middleton, *The Witch*, ed. Schafer (London: A. & C. Black, 1994), p. xi.
13. Baldwin Maxwell, *Studies in Beaumont and Fletcher* (Chapel Hill, NC: University of North Carolina Press, 1939), 143.
14. Schafer, 'Introduction', p. xiv.
15. A. A. Bromham, 'The Date of *The Witch* and the Essex Divorce Case', *Notes and Queries*, 225 (1980), 149–52; Anne Lancashire, '*The Witch*: Stage Flop or Political Mistake?', in Kenneth Friedenreich (ed.), *'Accompaninge the Players'*: *Essays Celebrating Thomas Middleton, 1580–1980* (New York: AMS Press, 1983), 161–81.
16. Brooke, 'Introduction', 58.
17. Schafer, 'Introduction', p. xiii.
18. Garry Wills, *Witches and Jesuits: Shakespeare's 'Macbeth'* (New York: Oxford University Press, 1995); Alastair Bellany, *The Politics of Court Scandal in Early Modern England: News Culture and the Overbury Affair, 1603–1660* (Cambridge: Cambridge University Press, 2002).
19. Taylor and Jowett, *Shakespeare Reshaped*, 107–236.
20. Richard Dutton, *Mastering the Revels: The Regulation and Censorship of English Renaissance Drama* (Iowa City: University of Iowa Press, 1991), 194; Janet Clare, *'Art made tongue-tied by authority'*: *Elizabethan and Jacobean Dramatic Censorship*, 2nd edn. (Manchester: Manchester University Press, 1999), 179.
21. Rasmussen, 'Shakespeare's Hand'; 'Reply to MacD. P. Jackson'.
22. Jackson, 'The Additions to *"The Second Maiden's Tragedy"*'.
23. Dutton, *Mastering the Revels*, 196.
24. Clare, *'Art made tongue-tied by authority'*, 181, 182.
25. Dutton, *Mastering the Revels*, 198–9.
26. Swapan Chakravorty, *Society and Politics in the Plays of Thomas Middleton* (Oxford: Clarendon Press, 1996), 22.
27. Mark Hutchings, '*Richard III* and *The Changeling*', *Notes and Queries*, 250 (2005), 229–30.
28. Scott McMillin, 'Acting and Violence: *The Revenger's Tragedy* and its Departures from *Hamlet*', *Studies in English Literature*, 24 (1984), 285.
29. Ibid.
30. Inga-Stina Ewbank, 'The Middle of Middleton', in Murray Biggs *et al.* (eds.), *The Arts of Performance in Elizabethan and Early Stuart Drama* (Edinburgh: Edinburgh University Press, 1991), 167.
31. Ibid. 168.
32. T. S. Eliot, 'Thomas Middleton', in *Elizabethan Dramatists* (London: Faber, 1963), 83–93.
33. Gary Taylor, 'Forms of Opposition: Shakespeare and Middleton',

*English Literary Renaissance*, 24 (1994), 283–314.

## CHAPTER 5

1. R. H., Barker, *Thomas Middleton* (London: Oxford University Press, 1958), 100.
2. R. V. Holdsworth, 'Introduction', in Thomas Middleton, *A Fair Quarrel*, ed. R. V. Holdsworth (London: Ernest Benn, 1974), p. xxii.
3. D. J. Lake, *The Canon of Thomas Middleton's Plays* (Cambridge: Cambridge University Press, 1975), 198–200.
4. Catherine M. Shaw, 'Introduction', in Thomas Middleton and William Rowley, *The Old Law*, ed. Shaw (New York: Garland Publishing, 1982), p. xxv.
5. Lake, *The Canon of Thomas Middleton's Plays*, 206–8.
6. Michael E. Mooney, '"Framing" as Collaborative Technique: Two Middleton–Rowley Plays', *Comparative Drama*, 13 (1979), 127–41; Richard L. Nochimson '"Sharing" *The Changeling* by Playwrights and Professors: The Certainty of Uncertain Knowledge about Collaborations', *Early Theatre*, 5 (2001), 37–55.
7. Mooney, '"Framing" as Collaborative Technique'; Holdsworth, 'Introduction'.
8. Charles Cathcart, 'Plural Authorship, Attribution, and the Children of the King's Revels', *Renaissance Forum*, 4 (2000), 11.
9. George E. Rowe, Jr, *Thomas Middleton and the New Comedy Tradition* (Lincoln, Neb.: University of Nebraska Press, 1979), 175.
10. Ibid. 181.
11. Ibid. 189.
12. Mooney, '"Framing" as Collaborative Technique', 132.
13. Nochimson, '"Sharing" *The Changeling* by Playwrights and Professors', 50.
14. Christopher Ricks, 'The Moral and Poetic Structure of *The Changeling*', *Essays in Criticism*, 10 (1960), 290–306.
15. Richard Dutton, 'Introduction', in Thomas Middleton, *'Women Beware Women' and Other Plays*, ed. Dutton (Oxford: Oxford University Press, 1999), pp. xxviii–xxx.
16. Mooney, '"Framing" as Collaborative Technique', 133.
17. Michael Scott, *Renaissance Drama and the Modern Audience* (Basingstoke: Macmillan, 1982), 84.
18. John Jowett, 'Introduction', in William Shakespeare, *Timon of Athens*, ed. John Jowett (London: Thomas Nelson & Sons, 2004), 132–53.

## CHAPTER 6

1. John Jowett, 'Varieties of Collaboration in Shakespeare's Problem Plays and Late Plays', in Richard Dutton and Jean E. Howard (eds.), *A Companion to Shakespeare's Works IV: The Poems, Problem Comedies, Late Plays* (Oxford: Blackwell, 2003), 117.
2. Mark Hutchings, '*Richard III* and *The Changeling*', *Notes and Queries*, 250 (2005), 229–30.
3. Martin Wiggins, *Journeymen in Murder: The Assassin in English Renaissance Drama* (Oxford: Clarendon Press, 1991), 188, 190.
4. Martin Butler, *Theatre and Crisis 1632–1642* (Cambridge: Cambridge University Press, 1984), 106–7.
5. John Marston, *Selected Plays*, ed. MacDonald P. Jackson and Michael O'Neill (Cambridge: Cambridge University Press, 1986), 329n.
6. Thomas L. Berger, 'The Petrarchan Fortress in *The Changeling*', *Renaissance Papers* (1969), 37–46.
7. T. H. McAlindon, *English Renaissance Tragedy* (London: Macmillan, 1986), 196.
8. Zara Bruzzi, ' "I find myself vnparadis'd": The Integrity of Daniel's *Delia*', *Cahiers Élisabéthains*, 48 (1995), 12.
9. A. A. Bromham and Zara Bruzzi, '*The Changeling* and the Years of Crisis 1619–1624: A Hieroglyph of Britain* (London: Pinter, 1990), 13–15.
10. Alan C. Dessen, and Leslie Thomson, *A Dictionary of Stage Directions in English Drama, 1580–1642* (Cambridge: Cambridge University Press, 1999), 115.
11. Grace Ioppolo, 'Sexual Treason, Treasonous Sexuality, and the Eventful Politics of James I in Middleton's *Hengist, King of Kent*', *Ben Jonson Journal*, 3 (1996), 88.

## AFTERWORD

1. John Jowett, 'Varieties of Collaboration in Shakespeare's Problem Plays and Late Plays', in Richard Dutton and Jean E. Howard (eds.), *A Companion to Shakespeare's Works IV: The Poems, Problem Comedies, Late Plays* (Oxford: Blackwell, 2003), 115.
2. Ibid.

# Select Bibliography

## MIDDLETON

### Editions of Single Plays

*A Fair Quarrel*, ed. R. V. Holdsworth (London: Ernest Benn, 1974).
*Women Beware Women*, ed. J. R. Mulryne (London: Methuen, 1975).
*The Second Maiden's Tragedy*, ed. Anne Lancashire (Manchester: Manchester University Press, 1978).
*A Game at Chess*, ed. T. H. Howard-Hill (Manchester: Manchester University Press, 1993).
*The Witch*, ed. Elizabeth Schafer (London: A. & C. Black, 1994).
*Women Beware Women*, ed. William C. Carroll, 2nd edn. (London: A. & C. Black, 1994).
*The Triumphs of Truth*, in *Jacobean City Pageants*, ed. Richard Dutton (Keele: Keele University Press, 1995).
*Hengist King of Kent, Or The Mayor of Queenborough*, ed. Grace Ioppolo (Malone Society; Oxford: Oxford University Press, 2003).

### Collections

*The Works of Thomas Middleton*, ed. A. H. Bullen (8 vols.; London: John C. Nimmo, 1885–6); vii. *City Pageants*.
*Thomas Middleton: Five Plays*, ed. Bryan Loughrey and Neil Taylor (London: Penguin, 1988). Includes *A Trick to Catch the Old One*; *The Revenger's Tragedy*; *A Chaste Maid in Cheapside*; *Women Beware Women*; *The Changeling*.
Middleton, Thomas, *'A Mad World, My Masters' and Other Plays*, ed. Michael Taylor (Oxford: Oxford University Press, 1995). Includes *A Mad World, My Masters*; *Michaelmas Term*; *A Trick to Catch the Old One*; *No Wit, No Help Like A Woman's*.
*Plays on Women*, ed. Kathleen McLuskie and David Bevington (Manchester: Manchester University Press, 1999). Includes *The Roaring Girl*; *A Chaste Maid in Cheapside*.

Middleton, Thomas, *'Women Beware Women' and Other Plays*, ed. Richard Dutton (Oxford: Oxford University Press, 1999). Includes *A Chaste Maid in Cheapside; Women Beware Women; The Changeling; A Game of Chess*.

## COLLABORATIONS

### Middleton and Dekker

*The Roaring Girl*, ed. Paul Mulholland (Manchester: Manchester University Press, 1987).
*The Roaring Girl*, ed. Elizabeth Cook (London: A. & C. Black, 1997).

### Middleton and Rowley

*The Old Law*, ed. Catherine M. Shaw (New York: Garland Publishing, 1982).
*The Changeling*, ed. Joost Daalder, 2nd edn. (London, A. & C. Black, 1990).
*The Changeling*, ed. N. W Bawcutt (Manchester: Manchester University Press, 1998).

### Middleton and Shakespeare

*A Yorkshire Tragedy*, ed. A. C. Cawley and Barry Gaines (Manchester: Manchester University Press, 1986).
*Timon of Athens*, ed. John Jowett (London: Thomas Nelson & Sons, 2004).

## OTHER PRIMARY WRITERS

Barker, Howard, and Middleton, Thomas, *Women Beware Women* (London: John Calder, 1989).
Daniel, Samuel, *The Complaint of Rosamond*, in *Elizabethan Verse Romances*, ed. M. M. Reese (London: Routledge, 1968).
Dekker, Thomas, *The Gull's Hornbook*, ed. R. B. McKerrow (London: De La More Press, 1904).
—— *The Dramatic Works of Thomas Dekker*, ed. Fredson Bowers (Cambridge: Cambridge University Press, 1953–61), ii.
Marlowe, Christopher, *Tamburlaine*, ed. J. S. Cunningham (Manchester: Manchester University Press, 1981).
Marston, John, *The Dutch Courtesan*, ed. Gamini Salgado (London:

Penguin, 1975).
—— *Selected Plays*, ed. MacDonald P. Jackson and Michael O'Neill (Cambridge: Cambridge University Press, 1986).
Shakespeare, William, *The Complete Works*, ed. Stanley Wells *et al.* (Oxford: Clarendon Press, 1986).
—— *Macbeth*, ed. Nicholas Brooke (Oxford: Oxford University Press, 1990).
—— *The Norton Shakespeare. Based on the Oxford Edition*, ed. Stephen Greenblatt *et al.* (New York: W. W. Norton & Company, 1997).

## FILM

*Revenger's Tragedy*, dir. Alex Cox (UK, 2002).

## SECONDARY CRITICISM

### Middleton

Barker, R. H., *Thomas Middleton* (London: Oxford University Press, 1958).
Berger, Thomas L., 'The Petrarchan Fortress in *The Changeling*', *Renaissance Papers* (1969), 37–46.
Briggs, Julia, 'Middleton's Forgotten Tragedy, *Hengist, King of Kent*', *Review of English Studies*, 41 (1990), 479–95.
Bromham, A. A., 'The Date of *The Witch* and the Essex Divorce Case', *Notes and Queries*, 225 (1980), 149–52.
—— 'Thomas Middleton's *The Triumphs of Truth*: City Politics in 1613', *The Seventeenth Century*, 10 (1995), 1–25.
—— and Bruzzi, Zara, *'The Changeling' and the Years of Crisis 1619–1624: A Hieroglyph of Britain* (London: Pinter, 1990).
Brooke, Nicholas, *Horrid Laughter in Jacobean Tragedy* (London: Open Books, 1979).
Brooks, John B., 'Recent Studies in Middleton', *English Literary Renaissance*, 14 (1984), 114–28.
Bruzzi, Zara, '"I find myself vnparadis'd": The Integrity of Daniel's *Delia*', *Cahiers Élisabéthains*, 48 (1995), 1–15.
—— 'A Device to Fit the Times: Intertextual Allusion in Thomas Middleton's *Women Beware Women*', in Michele Marrapodi and A. J. Hoenselaars (eds.), *The Italian World of English Renaissance Drama: Cultural Exchange and Intertextuality* (Newark, Del.: University of Delaware Press, 1998), 302–20.

Chakravorty, Swapan, *Society and Politics in the Plays of Thomas Middleton* (Oxford: Clarendon Press, 1996).
Comensoli, Viviana, 'Merchants and Madcaps: Dekker's *Honest Whore* Plays and the *Commedia dell'arte*', in Michele Marrapodi *et al.* (eds.), *Shakespeare's Italy: Functions of Italian Locations in Renaissance Drama* (Manchester: Manchester University Press, 1993), 125–39.
Dynes, William R., 'The Trickster Figure in Jacobean City Comedy', *Studies in English Literature*, 33 (1993), 365–84.
Eliot, T. S., 'Thomas Middleton', in *Elizabethan Dramatists* (London: Faber, 1963), 83–93.
Ewbank, Inga-Stina, 'The Middle of Middleton', in Murray Biggs *et al.* (eds.), *The Arts of Performance in Elizabethan and Early Stuart Drama* (Edinburgh: Edinburgh University Press, 1991), 156–72.
Garber, Marjorie, 'The Logic of the Transvestite', in David Scott Kastan and Peter Stallybrass (eds.), *Staging the Renaissance: Reinterpretations of Elizabethan and Jacobean Drama* (London: Routledge, 1991), 221–34.
Taylor, Gary, 'Middleton, Thomas (bap. 1580, d. 1627)', *Oxford Dictionary of National Biography* (Oxford: Oxford University Press, 2004; online edn, 2006: http://www.oxforddnb.com/view/article/18682).
Gasper, Julia, *The Dragon and the Dove: The Plays of Thomas Dekker* (Oxford: Clarendon Press, 1990).
Gibbons, Brian, *Jacobean City Comedy: A Study of Satiric Plays by Jonson, Marston and Middleton*, 2nd edn. (London: Methuen, 1980).
Heinemann, Margot, *Puritanism and Theatre: Thomas Middleton and Opposition Drama under the Early Stuarts* (Cambridge: Cambridge University Press, 1980).
Hope, Jonathan, *The Authorship of Shakespeare's Plays: A Socio-Linguistic Study* (Cambridge: Cambridge University Press, 1994).
Howard, Jean E., 'Crossdressing, the Theatre, and Gender Struggle in Early Modern England', *Shakespeare Quarterly*, 39 (1988), 418–40.
—— 'Sex and Social Conflict: The Erotics of *The Roaring Girl*', in Susan Zimmerman, (ed.), *Erotic Politics: Desire on the Renaissance Stage* (London: Routledge, 1992), 170–90.
—— *The Stage and Social Struggle in Early Modern England* (London: Routledge, 1994).
Hutchings, Mark, 'Anti-Theatrical Prejudice and *1 Honest Whore*', *Notes and Queries*, 250 (2005), 220–1.
—— '*Richard III* and *The Changeling*', *Notes and Queries*, 250 (2005), 229–30.
Ioppolo, Grace, 'Sexual Treason, Treasonous Sexuality, and the Eventful Politics of James I in Middleton's *Hengist, King of Kent*', *Ben Jonson Journal*, 3 (1996), 87–107.
Jackson, MacDonald P., *Studies in Attribution: Middleton and Shakespeare* (Salzburg Studies in English Literature: Jacobean Drama Studies 39;

Salzburg: Institut für Sprache und Literatur, Universität Salzburg, 1979).
—— 'The Additions to *"The Second Maiden's Tragedy"*: Shakespeare or Middleton?', *Shakespeare Quarterly*, 41 (1990), 402–5.
Jowett, John, 'Thomas Middleton', in Arthur F. Kinney (ed.), *A Companion to Renaissance Drama* (Oxford: Blackwell, 2002), 507–23.
Lake, D. J., *The Canon of Thomas Middleton's Plays* (Cambridge: Cambridge University Press, 1975).
Lancashire, Anne, '*The Witch*: Stage Flop or Political Mistake?', in Kenneth Friedenreich (ed.), *'Accompaninge the Players'*: *Essays Celebrating Thomas Middleton, 1580–1980* (New York: AMS Press, 1983), 161–81.
Leinwand, Theodore B., *The City Staged: Jacobean Comedy, 1603–1613* (Madison, Wis.: University of Wisconsin Press, 1986).
Levin, Richard, *The Multiple Plot in English Renaissance Drama* (Madison, Wis.: University of Wisconsin Press, 1971).
Limon, Jerzy, *Dangerous Matter: English Drama and Politics 1623/24* (Cambridge: Cambridge University Press, 1986).
McAlindon, T. H., *English Renaissance Tragedy* (London: Macmillan, 1986).
McLuskie, Kathleen E., *Dekker and Heywood* (Basingstoke: Macmillan, 1994).
McMillin, Scott, 'Acting and Violence: *The Revenger's Tragedy* and its Departures from *Hamlet*', *Studies in English Literature*, 24 (1984), 275–91.
Mulholland, Paul, 'The Date of *The Roaring Girl*', *Review of English Studies*, 28 (1977), 18–31.
Mulryne, J. R., *Thomas Middleton* (Writers and their Work Series; Harlow: Longman, 1979).
Orgel, Stephen, 'The Subtexts of *The Roaring Girl*', in Susan Zimmerman (ed.), *Erotic Politics: Desire on the Renaissance Stage* (London: Routledge, 1992), 12–26.
Rasmussen, Eric, 'Shakespeare's Hand in *"The Second Maiden's Tragedy"*', *Shakespeare Quarterly*, 40 (1989), 1–26.
—— 'Reply to MacD. P. Jackson', *Shakespeare Quarterly*, 41 (1990), 406–7.
Ribner, Irving, *Jacobean Tragedy: The Quest for Moral Order* (London: Methuen, 1962; repr. 1979).
Ricks, Christopher, 'The Moral and Poetic Structure of *The Changeling*', *Essays in Criticism*, 10 (1960), 290–306.
Rose, Mary Beth, 'Women in Men's Clothes: Apparel and Social Stability in *The Roaring Girl*', *English Literary Renaissance*, 14 (1984), 367–91; repr. in Arthur F. Kinney and Dan S. Collins (eds), *Renaissance Historicism: Selections from 'English Literary Renaissance'* (Amherst, Mass.: University of Massachusetts Press, 1987), 223–47.

Rowe, George E., Jr, *Thomas Middleton and the New Comedy Tradition* (Lincoln, Neb.: University of Nebraska Press, 1979).
Stachniewski, John, 'Calvinist Psychology in Middleton's Tragedies', in R. V. Holdsworth (ed.), *Three Jacobean Revenge Tragedies* (Basingstoke: Macmillan, 1990), 226–46.
Steen, Sara Jane, *Ambrosia in an Earthern Vessel: Three Centuries of Audience and Reader Response to the Works of Thomas Middleton* (New York: AMS Press, 1993).
Taylor, Gary, 'Forms of Opposition: Shakespeare and Middleton', *English Literary Renaissance*, 24 (1994), 283–314.
—— and Jowett, John, *Shakespeare Reshaped 1606–1623* (Oxford: Clarendon Press, 1993).
White, Martin, *Middleton and Tourneur* (Basingstoke: Macmillan, 1992).
Wiggins, Martin, *Journeymen in Murder: The Assassin in English Renaissance Drama* (Oxford: Clarendon Press, 1991).

## Collaboration

Barthes, Roland, 'The Death of the Author' (1968), in *Image – Music – Text*, ed. and trans. Stephen Heath (London: Fontana, 1977), 142–8.
—— 'From Work to Text' (1971), in *Image – Music –Text*, ed. and trans. Stephen Heath (London: Fontana, 1977), 155–64.
Bentley, G. E., *The Profession of Dramatist in Shakespeare's Time, 1590–1642* (Princeton: Princeton University Press, 1971).
Brooks, Douglas A., *From Playhouse to Printing House: Drama and Authorship in Early Modern England* (Cambridge: Cambridge University Press, 2000).
Cathcart, Charles, 'Plural Authorship, Attribution, and the Children of the King's Revels', *Renaissance Forum*, 4/2 (2000), n.p.
Clark, Sandra, *The Plays of Beaumont and Fletcher: Sexual Themes and Dramatic Representation* (Hemel Hempstead: Harvester, 1994).
Foucault, Michel, 'What is an Author?' (1969), in Paul Rabinow (ed.), *The Foucault Reader: An Introduction to Foucault's Thought*, trans. Josue V. Harari (London: Penguin, 1991), 101–20.
Ioppolo, Grace, 'The Transmission of an English Renaissance Play-Text', in Arthur F. Kinney (ed.), *A Companion to Renaissance Drama* (Oxford: Blackwell, 2002), 163–79.
Jowett, John, 'Varieties of Collaboration in Shakespeare's Problem Plays and Late Plays', in Richard Dutton and Jean E. Howard (eds.), *A Companion to Shakespeare's Works IV: The Poems, Problem Comedies, Late Plays* (Oxford: Blackwell, 2003), 106–28.
McMullan, Gordon, *The Politics of Unease in the Plays of John Fletcher* (Amherst, Mass.: University of Massachusetts Press, 1994).
Masten, Jeffrey A., 'Playwrighting: Authorship and Collaboration', in

John D. Cox and David Scott Kastan (eds.), *A New History of Early English Drama* (New York: Columbia University Press, 1997), 357–82.
—— *Textual Intercourse: Collaboration, Authorship, and Sexualities in Renaissance Drama* (Cambridge: Cambridge University Press, 1997).
Maxwell, Baldwin, *Studies in Beaumont and Fletcher* (Chapel Hill, NC: University of North Carolina Press, 1939).
Mooney, Michel E., ' "Framing" as Collaborative Technique: Two Middleton–Rowley Plays', *Comparative Drama*, 13 (1979), 127–41.
Nochimson, Richard L., ' "Sharing" *The Changeling* by Playwrights and Professors: The Certainty of Uncertain Knowledge about Collaborations', *Early Theatre*, 5 (2001), 37–55.
Orgel, Stephen, 'What is a Text?' (1981), in David Scott Kastan and Peter Stallybrass (eds.), *Staging the Renaissance: Reinterpretations of Elizabethan and Jacobean Drama* (London: Routledge, 1991), 83–7.
Street, R. J., and Giles, H., 'Speech Accommodation Theory: A Social and Cognitive Approach to Language and Speech Behaviour', in Michael E. Roloff and Charles R. Berger (eds.), *Social Cognition and Communication* (Beverly Hills, Calif.: Sage Publications, 1982).
Vickers, Brian, *Shakespeare, Co-Author: A Historical Study of Five Collaborative Plays* (Oxford: Oxford University Press, 2002).

## General

Bakhtin, M. M., *Speech Genres and Other Late Essays*, ed. Caryl Emerson and Michael Holquist, trans. Vern W. McGee (Austin, Tex.: University of Texas Press, 1986).
Beier, A. L., and Finlay, Roger, *London 1500–1700: The Making of the Metropolis* (London: Longman, 1986).
Bellany, Alastair, *The Politics of Court Scandal in Early Modern England: News Culture and the Overbury Affair, 1603–1660* (Cambridge: Cambridge University Press, 2002).
Benjamin, Walter, 'Paris, Capital of the Nineteenth Century', in Peter Demetz (ed.), *Reflections: Essays, Aphorisms, Autobiographical Writings*, trans. Edmund Jephcott (New York: Schocken Books, 1978), 146–62.
Bentley, G. E., *The Jacobean and Caroline Stage* 7 vols. (Oxford: Clarendon Press, 1941–68).
Brenner, Robert, *Merchants and Revolution: Commercial Change, Political Conflict, and London's Overseas Traders, 1550–1653* (Princeton: Princeton University Press, 1993).
Butler, Martin, *Theatre and Crisis 1632–1642* (Cambridge: Cambridge University Press, 1984).
Clare, Janet, *'Art made tongue-tied by authority': Elizabethan and Jacobean Dramatic Censorship*, 2nd edn. (Manchester: Manchester University Press, 1999).

Cressy, David, 'Gender Trouble and Cross-Dressing in Early Modern England', *Journal of British Studies*, 35 (1996), 438–65.
Dessen, Alan C., and Thomson, Leslie, *A Dictionary of Stage Directions in English Drama, 1580–1642* (Cambridge: Cambridge University Press, 1999).
Dillon, Janette, 'Fashion, Nation and Theatre in Late Sixteenth-Century London', in Edward J. Esche (ed.), *Shakespeare and his Contemporaries in Performance* (London: Ashgate, 2000), 161–76.
Dutton, Richard, *Mastering the Revels: The Regulation and Censorship of English Renaissance Drama* (Iowa City: University of Iowa Press, 1991).
Greenblatt, Stephen, *Shakespearean Negotiations: The Circulation of Social Energy* (Oxford: Clarendon Press, 1988).
Gurr, Andrew, *The Shakespearean Stage 1574–1642*, 3rd edn. (Cambridge: Cambridge University Press, 1992).
—— 'The Authority of the Globe and the Fortune', in Lena Cowen Orlin (ed.), *Material London, Ca. 1600* (Philadelphia: University of Pennsylvania Press, 2000), 251–67.
—— *The Shakespeare Company, 1594–1642* (Cambridge: Cambridge University Press, 2004).
Hattaway, Michael, 'Drama and Society', in A. R. Braunmuller and Michael Hattaway (eds.), *The Cambridge Companion to Renaissance Drama* (Cambridge: Cambridge University Press, 2003), 93–130.
Henslowe, Philip, *Henslowe's Diary*, ed. R. A. Foakes, 2nd edn. (Cambridge: Cambridge University Press, 2002).
Jardine, Lisa, *Still Harping on Daughters: Women and Drama in the Age of Shakespeare* (Brighton: Harvester Press, 1983).
Kastan, David Scott, and Stallybrass, Peter (eds.), *Staging the Renaissance: Reinterpretations of Elizabethan and Jacobean Drama* (London: Routledge, 1991).
Knowles, James, 'The Spectacle of the Realm: Civic Consciousness, Rhetoric and Ritual in Early Modern London', in J. R. Mulryne and Margaret Shewring (eds.), *Theatre and Government under the Early Stuarts* (Cambridge: Cambridge University Press, 1993), 157–89.
Levin, Richard, 'Women in the Renaissance Theatre Audience', *Shakespeare Quarterly*, 40 (1989), 165–74.
Lindley, David, *The Trials of Frances Howard: Fact and Fiction at the Court of King James* (London: Routledge, 1993).
Manley, Laurence, *Literature and Culture in Early Modern London* (Cambridge: Cambridge University Press, 1995).
Mullaney, Steven, *The Place of the Stage: License, Play, and Power in Renaissance England* (Chicago: University of Chicago Press, 1988).
Parry, Graham, *The Golden Age Restored: The Culture of the Stuart Court, 1603–42* (Manchester: Manchester University Press, 1981).

Orgel, Stephen, *Impersonations: The Performance of Gender in Shakespeare's England* (Cambridge: Cambridge University Press, 1996).

Prestwich, Menna, *Cranfield: Politics and Profits under the Early Stuarts* (Oxford: Clarendon Press, 1966).

Salingar, Leo, 'Jacobean Playwrights and "Judicious" Spectators', *Renaissance Drama*, 22 (1991), 209–34.

Scott, Michael, *Renaissance Drama and the Modern Audience* (Basingstoke: Macmillan, 1982).

Stallybrass, Peter, 'Worn Worlds: Clothes and Identity on the Renaissance Stage', in Margreta de Grazia *et al.* (eds.), *Subject and Object in Renaissance Culture* (Cambridge: Cambridge University Press, 1996), 289–320.

Tilley, Morris Palmer, *A Dictionary of the Proverbs in England in the Sixteenth and Seventeenth Centuries* (Ann Arbor: University of Michigan Press, 1950).

Tricomi, A.H., *Anti-Court Drama in England, 1603–42* (Charlottesville, Va.: University Press of Virginia, 1989).

Twyning, John, *London Dispossessed: Literature and Social Space in the Early Modern City* (Basingstoke: Macmillan, 1998).

Wills, Garry, *Witches and Jesuits: Shakespeare's 'Macbeth'* (New York: Oxford University Press, 1995).

Zimmerman, Susan (ed.), *Erotic Politics: Desire on the Renaissance Stage* (London: Routledge, 1992).

# Index

Accommodation theory, 35, 75
Authorship, 25–6, 28, 29, 30, 31, 32, 33, 34, 35, 99

Bakhtin, Mikhail, 99
Barker, Howard, 98
Barker, Richard Hindry, 73, 96
Barthes, Roland, 26, 36, 36
Beaumont and Fletcher Folio, 73
Bedlam or Bethlehem Hospital, 43
Bellany, Alistair, 17
Benjamin, Walter, 49
Bentley, G.E., 2, 31, 32
Bodley, Sir Thomas, 29
Brecht, Bertolt, 37
Brooke, Nicholas, 63
Bruzzi, Zara, 21, 96
Buc, Sir George, 65
Burbage, Richard, 68, 70
Butler, Martin, 90

Calvinism, 22
Carr, Robert, Viscount Rochester, Earl of Somerset, 14–16, 17, 21–2, 63
Cathcart, Charles, 75

Cecil, Robert, 15
Censorship, 23–4, 28, 64, 65
Charles, Prince of Wales, 14, 17
Clifford, Rosamond, 93
Coke, Sir Edward, Lord Chief Justice, 16
Coleridge, Samuel Taylor, 53
Commedia dell'arte, 42
Companies:
  The Admiral's/Prince Henry's Men, 37, 40, 51
  The Chamberlain's/King's Men, 4, 29, 36, 40, 54, 55, 56, 58, 61, 63, 64, 65, 66, 67, 68, 70, 71, 74
  Lady Elizabeth's Men, 88–9
  Prince Charles's Men, 74
  The Children of Paul's, 40
  Queen's Revels, 74, 88
  Worcester's Men, 37, 40
*Consistory of London Correction Book*, 44, 50, 51, 52
Cox, Alex, 98
Crosse, Henry, *Vertues Commonwealth*, 42

Daniel, Samuel, 88
  *The Complaint of Rosamond*, 92–6
Day, John, 74

119

# INDEX

Dekker, Thomas, 4, 37–9;
  *The Belman of London*, 45
  *Caesar's Fall* (with
    Middleton, Munday,
    Drayton, Webster), 39
  *The Four Birds of Noah's Ark*,
    40
  *The Gull's Hornbook*, 1, 49
  *Lantern and Candlelight*, 45
  *The Meeting of Gallants at an*
    *Ordinary* (with
    Middleton), 39
  *News from Gravesend* (with
    Middleton), 39
  *Old Fortunatus*, 39
  *The Shoemaker's Holiday*, 40
  *Troia Nova Triumphans*, 39
  *The Whore of Babylon*, 40
  *The Witch of Edmonton*
    (with Ford and William),
    74
  *The Wonderful Year*, 40
Drayton, Michael, 37
Dynes, William R., 10

Eliot, T. S., 3, 36, 70
Elizabeth, Princess, daughter
  of James I, 91, 96

*Flaneur*, 49–50
Fleay, F.G., 56
Fletcher, John, 37
  *The Nice Valour*, 64
Ford, John, 37, 73
Foucault, Michel, 26, 36
Frederick, Elector Palatine,
  husband of Princess
  Elizabeth, 17, 91, 96
Frith, Mary, 44

Greenblatt, Stephen, 36
Greene, Robert, 37
Gunpowder Plot, 16, 64

Hafler, Max, 80
Hannay, Patrick, *Sheretine and*
  *Mariana*, 96
Hattaway, Michael, 8
Heinemann, Margot, 23
Henri IV, King of France, 66
Henry II, King of England,
  93, 95
Henslowe, Philip, 2, 27 35, 37,
  39, 41, 58
Heywood, Thomas, 37, 73
Holdsworth, R.V., 73, 75
Holinshed, Raphael, 61
Holmes, Sean, 80
Howard, Frances, Countess of
  Essex, Countess of
  Somerset, 16, 17, 19, 21, 24,
  66, 96

Jackson, Macdonald P., 75
James I, King of England, 3,
  14, 15, 18, 61, 63, 62, 65, 66,
  71, 96
  *Demonology*, 61
Jones, Richard, printer, 32
Jonson, Ben, 29, 30, 32, 33, 98;
  *Every Man Out of His*
    *Humour*, 29
  *Workes*, 29, 30
Jowett, John, 87, 99

Knight, Charles, 56
Knowles, James, 13

Lake, D. J., 73, 75
Lancashire, Anne, 18

# INDEX

London, 1, 3, 5–14, 20, 40, 41, 47
Lumley, Sir Martin, 13

*The Magnificent Entertainment*, 39
Marlowe, Christopher, 2, 32, 33, 35, 37, 98
  *Tamburlaine*, 32
  *Doctor Faustus*, 35
Marston, John, *The Dutch Courtesan*, 88–91
Massinger, Philip, 37
Masten, Jeffrey, 31
Master of the Revels, 28, 31, 65
Middleton, Thomas,
  *Anything for a Quiet Life*, 24
  *The Black Book*, 6, 40
  *The Bloody Banquet* (with Dekker), 39
  *The Changeling*, (with Rowley), 3, 24, 41, 43, 67, 73, 74, 75, 77, 79, 82, 83, 84, 85, 88, 89, 91–7
  *A Chaste Maid in Cheapside*, 7, 8, 22, 23, 45, 47
  *A Fair Quarrel* (with Rowley), 69, 73, 74, 75, 77, 78, 79, 82
  *Father Hubbard's Tales*, 6
  *A Game at Chess*, 3, 17, 18, 19, 24, 57, 74, 92, 96
  *The Ghost of Lucrece*, 67, 92
  *Hengist, King of Kent*, 14, 17, 18, 19, 69, 85, 92, 96, 97
  *1 Honest Whore* (with Dekker), 39, 41–6, 83
  *Inner Temple Masque*, 74
  *The Lady's Tragedy (The Second Maiden's Tragedy)*, 17, 18, 24, 55, 56, 65, 66, 68, 92
  *A Mad World, My Masters*, 89, 96
  *Michaelmas Term*, 7
  *Microcynicon*, 6
  *More Dissemblers Besides Women*, 17, 18, 19, 22, 69, 77, 82, 92
  *No Wit, No Help Like a Woman's*, 9–10, 11–12
  *The Old Law* (with Rowley and Massinger/Heywood?), 7, 24, 61, 73–5, 77, 79–82, 85
  *The Phoenix*, 6, 41, 64, 81
  *The Puritan*, 47
  *Randall, Earl of Chester*, 37
  *The Revenger's Tragedy*, 6, 15, 17, 20, 23, 41, 43, 56, 57, 59–61, 65, 67, 68, 78, 85, 88, 92, 96
  *The Roaring Girl* (with Dekker), 39, 44–53, 78
  *The Spanish Gypsy* (with Dekker, Ford and Rowley), 39, 73
  *A Trick to Catch the Old One*, 8, 9, 40, 45, 47
  *The Triumphs of Honour and Industry*, 13
  *The Triumphs of Integrity*, 13, 14
  *The Triumphs of Truth*, 12, 13, 23, 39
  *The Witch*, 17, 19, 24, 56, 61, 62, 63, 65, 66, 67, 77, 82
  *The Widow*, 45
  *Wit at Several Weapons* (with

# INDEX

Rowley), 73
*Women Beware Women*, 6, 15, 17, 19, 20, 22, 23, 92, 93, 95, 96, 97
*The World Tossed at Tennis* (with Rowley), 14, 73, 74
*A Yorkshire Tragedy*, 55, 56
*Your Five Gallants*, 9
Middleton, Sir Thomas (Lord Mayor 1613–14), 12, 14
Mooney, Michael E., 74, 75, 77, 82
Munday, Anthony, 37

National Theatre, 83
Nochimson, Richard L., 74, 75, 82

Orange Tree Theatre, Richmond, 90
Orgel, Stephen, 32
Overbury, Sir Thomas, 16, 19, 96
Oxford Middleton, 74, 98

Palatinate, 22
Playhouses:
 The Fortune, 27, 50, 53
 The Globe, 26, 56, 70
 The Phoenix, 83
 The Rose, 2, 26, 27
Postmoderm theory, 25

Reynolds, John, 92
Ribner, Irving, 23
Roman New Comedy, 11, 78, 79, 80
Royal Exchange, 1
Royal Shakespeare Company (RSC), 80, 81

Rowe, George E. Jr., 80
Rowley, William, 4, 29, 37, 38, 73, 74

Scot, Reginald, 62
*A Discovery of Witchcraft*, 61
Seymour, William, 66
Shakespeare, William, 3, 4, 29, 30, 31, 36, 38 54–72, 98
 First Folio, 30, 36, 65, 71, 98
 *Hamlet*, 33, 67, 68, 69, 71
 *Henry VIII*, 56
 *King Lear*, 8, 33, 58, 60, 61
 *Macbeth*, 55, 56, 61, 62, 63, 65, 66, 67, 71
 *Measure for Measure*, 7, 43, 55, 56, 64, 65, 71, 81, 98
 *Much Ado About Nothing*, 91
 *Othello*, 91
 *Pericles*, 56
 *The Rape of Lucrece*, 67, 92, 94
 *Richard III*, 67, 68, 88
 *Timon of Athens* (with Middleton), 55, 56, 58–9, 87
 *Titus Andronicus*, 56
 *Twelfth Night*, 46
 *Two Noble Kinsmen*, 56
 *The Winter's Tale*, 91
Spain, 17, 18, 37, 40
Stuart, Arbella, 66
Stubbes, Philip, *The Anatomie of Abuses*, 44, 46
Sumptuary laws, 43–5, 48
Swetnam, Joseph, *The Arraignment of Lewd, Idle, Froward, and Unconstant Women*, 21

Taylor, Gary, 3, 70, 71
Taylor, Michael, 8
Trickster, 10–11, 15, 40

Villiers, George, Marquis,
    Duke, of Buckingham, 15,
    16, 21, 22

Walters, Sam, 90
Webster, John, 37
Wells, William, 56
Wiggins, Martin, 89
Wilkins, George, 74
Witchcraft, 16, 19, 61–4, 71

www.ingramcontent.com/pod-product-compliance
Lightning Source LLC
Chambersburg PA
CBHW030143240426
43672CB00005B/245